"So many people become victims of a traumatic event early in life, which adversely dictates how they deal with the rest of their life circumstances and opportunities. Micheline Nader's beautiful book provides easy-to-follow instructions on how to operate your reset button so that you can tap into divine consciousness and manifest all of your potential. The book's premise is supported by the most current awareness in biology, neurology, and epigenetics with a deep sharing from the author's own life and losses in growing up in Lebanon in the 1970s. *The Dolphin's Dance* is not just a compelling title but is woven into the entire book. Visualize a dolphin bounding out of the water and doing a joyous flip in a sparkling lagoon and you are on your way to understanding the permanent *joie de vivre* this book helps you attain."

—**David Mager**, Managing Member, Deepak Chopra Dream Weaver LLC

"At the root of what I see in patients sitting before me is a deep and penetrating story they carry that cuts them off from their potential to heal. As a doctor, I am always looking for ways to help my patients connect with their most powerful selves because I know, from that point, anything is possible. This is a challenge for most of us. To have a clear, concise, and gentle way to access this is a gift. *The Dolphin's Dance* is that gift and is the resource I will be sharing with my patients. It thoughtfully and carefully guides us through the layers that enshroud us and contribute to illness. Ms. Nader, through her ability to share her story and enlarge upon it, makes the road to self-awareness accessible."

—**Dr. Karen Koffler, MD,** Medical Director: Health & Wellness, Canyon Ranch Hotel & Spa

"Through the imagery and heart-felt stories of *The Dolphin's Dance*, Micheline takes the reader on a beautiful journey through the mysterious and often dark waters of the human mind. If you are ready to take responsibility for your life, heal your past, and step bravely and boldly into your amazing future, this book will set you on your path, using an extremely clear and easy-to-follow process. This is the perfect gift not only for yourself but for everyone you know!"

)r. **Sheri Rosenthal**, author of *The Complete Idiot's Guide to Toltec Wisdom* and *Banish Mind Spam!*

D0289685

"I read *The Dolphin's Dance* expecting to be educated and to gain insight as a medical professional; I gained this and more. I found myself personally enlightened, moved, and enriched! I wish I could write a prescription for this book for every woman and man who has experienced hurt, trauma, or serious disappointment, and setbacks as a result. It would go a long way towards lessening the burden on our mental healthcare system. I give this book my strongest recommendation."

—**Donnica L. Moore, MD**, President, Sapphire Women's Health Group; Editor in Chief of *Women's Health for Life*

"Micheline brings a clarity to the journey of transformation and healing by showing us how to look deeper into our own consciousness. The processes in the book show us how to gently be responsible for our own spiritual journey. Anyone can do these exercises! Give yourself the gift of making the time and taking the space to do them. Your soul will thank you! Micheline Nader is a generous and authentic example of the processes she presents. Her heart and soul are all over each page and her healing journey is deeply inspiring."

—**Rev. Frankie Timmers**, Spiritual Director, Center for Spiritual Living

"In our world today, many people do not follow a specific faith but do identify as spiritual. Micheline Nader's *The Dolphin's Dance* offers its readers a clear spiritual pathway for personal development in a complex material world. She offers, much like the '12 step' program, a way for those seeking spiritual development to detach from the material world. This book is an easy read, without a lot of classic dogma or rhetoric. I would encourage anyone wanting to start down their own spiritual path to dive deeply into this highly meaningful work."

—**Robert B. Rosenfeld**, Founder and CEO, Idea Connection Systems, Inc., author of *Making the Invisible Visible*

"The Dolphin's Dance offers not only a glimpse at the grandeur and mystery of being human but also actual steps to make more room in oneself for the vastness and depth of our humanity to inform our lives."

—**Gerard Senehi**, Master Mentalist, President and Founder, Open Future Institute

"When it comes to self-awareness, there are many great books from the masters that have inspired millions to embark on the quest for self-knowledge. When I read *The Dolphin's Dance*, I was intrigued that it offered not only inspiration but a step by step path to transformation and I was curious to see if the method applied to my own experience. I was struck by how much it does and how it conveys both the mystery of who we are but also very concrete steps to be more conscious of what makes us up, which in turns makes more room for who we really are and who we can become."

—**Francesca Rusciani**, Executive Director, Open Future Institute

"There are many books out there on the exploration of consciousness but *The Dolphin's Dance* has a wonderful unique voice, which elegantly leads the reader forward into their journey. Micheline Nader is a rock star who creates such a close and intimate connection with those she speaks to—and she spoke deeply to me."

—**Laurie Meadoff**, CEO, Laurie Inc. and Team

THE DOLPHIN'S DANCE

DISCOVER YOUR TRUE SELF THROUGH
A POWERFUL 5 STEP JOURNEY
INTO CONSCIOUS AWARENESS

MICHELINE NADER

BALBOA
PRESS
A DIVISION OF HAY HOUSE

Balboa Press books may be ordered through booksellers or by contacting:

Balboa Press
A Division of Hay House
1663 Liberty Drive
Bloomington, IN 47403
www.balboapress.com
1 (877) 407-4847

Because of the dynamic nature of the Internet, any web addresses or links contained in this book may have changed since publication and may no longer be valid. The views expressed in this work are solely those of the author and do not necessarily reflect the views of the publisher, and the publisher hereby disclaims any responsibility for them.

The author of this book does not dispense medical advice or prescribe the use of any technique as a form of treatment for physical, emotional, or medical problems without the advice of a physician, either directly or indirectly. The intent of the author is only to offer information of a general nature to help you in your quest for emotional and spiritual well-being. In the event you use any of the information in this book for yourself, which is your constitutional right, the author and the publisher assume no responsibility for your actions.

Any people depicted in stock imagery provided by Thinkstock are models, and such images are being used for illustrative purposes only. Certain stock imagery © Thinkstock.

Print information available on the last page.

ISBN: 978-1-5043-2645-2 (sc)
ISBN: 978-1-5043-2647-6 (hc)
ISBN: 978-1-5043-2646-9 (e)
Library of Congress Control Number: 2015900397

Balboa Press rev. date: 3/11/2015

To my parents, John and Valerie, who gave me the gift of life

Contents

ACKNOWLEDGMENTS

I would like to express my boundless love and gratitude to my three great dolphins: my husband Francois, my son Ralph, and my daughter Jessica. They have all been a constant source of infinite love, strength, and more during my creative journey, and Jessica also made an enormous contribution to the writing and editing of the book.

I am thankful to my special friends who walked by my side on my path of conscious awareness. I wish to express my deep appreciation to my editor Ellen Daly, who supported my writing adventure, as well as to my focus group, particularly Timothy Goddard, Frankie Timmers, Gerard Senehi, Francesca Rusciani, and Mino Dallosto, whose advice was essential to completing this work.

On my own journey, I have been inspired by many great spiritual masters, writers, philosophers, and psychologists, both ancient and contemporary, who have shared their precious knowledge about manifesting the life we want. They taught me about the law of attraction, quantum physics, energy healing, the law of cause and effect, karma, chakras, the power of positive thinking, the evolutionary impulse, the laws of the universe, and much more. I am grateful to all who have dedicated their lives to helping others understand the limitless aspects of the human mind and the human spirit and the effect of our thoughts in creating our reality.

Last but not least, I am grateful to the dolphins of the sea, to whom I owe my dream, my most spectacular spins, my transformation, my song, and my dance.

INTRODUCTION

The morning breeze feels different today. I am sixteen years old, sitting on a chair on our neighbor's balcony, surrounded by my cousins and friends in a small Christian village in the Lebanese mountains.

All eyes seem to be focused on me; my friends and cousins are attentive, their faces filled with sorrow and sympathy. The fall colors seem sharper, and the smell of the mountain is more intense, but my eyes are empty and my senses are numb.

I am thoroughly lost; I don't want to be here. Please take me somewhere I can hide. Somewhere I can digest what is happening. Please take me somewhere I can dream of a different reality.

Suddenly, the bells of the Catholic church ring as a prelude for an announcement, followed closely by the mosque's chant in the Muslim village below. We are accustomed to hearing this loud invocation at dawn and dusk, but today it is different: we are hearing it mid-morning. This voice that has acclaimed the big God (Allahou Akbar) is broadcasting the loss of my big God. It is calling the villagers to my dad's funeral.

Does this mean it is a done deal?

Big God, is it real?

And if you are so big, why are you allowing my young dad, just forty-two years old, to die?

Maybe it is not real?

Anyway, what does the big God of the Muslim village have to

do with my dad, a Christian? It may be someone else. I must have misheard the name …

While my mind is racing with questions, my stomach is tightening, and my throat feels restricted. I am trying to review the previous day's events in my head, but family and friends constantly interrupt me with acts of kindness. A friend tries to pour some milk into my mouth while reminding me that I have not eaten or drunk in the past twenty-four hours. I know I have not slept, either.

I try to close my eyes so that people will leave me alone and I can go back to my thoughts.

My dad, John, was the inspiration of my life, and I was his. Every day, I felt his unconditional love, and I never doubted myself, because he believed in me.

Who will I become without him?

And how did I manage to leave his bedside without saying good-bye?

Yesterday, at the same hour, I went to visit him at the hospital. He looked pale and had no energy, but as soon as he saw me, he had a smile on his red lips. Red—what was that liquid coming from his mouth? Was it blood?

My mom asked me to kiss my dad, and in that very moment, I felt that she was asking me to kiss him good-bye. Good-bye forever?

No way, I said to myself. Instead, I ran to the church and started praying to Santa Rita to solicit her healing power. This miraculous saint, who once healed my dying grandmother, could certainly heal my sick dad. After all, she and I became friends in my dream when I was twelve years old. She announced herself to me and told me that she was healing my grandma against all odds—and she did. How could she fail to honor my request this time?

I spent hours kneeling at the church's altar, pretty sure of my deal with my friend, the saint of the impossible.

Done deal, I thought to myself. Finally, I left the church and headed to my dear Aunt Nadia's house. She was waiting for me outside, wearing a purple and white dress, with a strange look in her eyes that I couldn't read.

She hugged me close. "Micheline, you must be strong now for your mom and younger siblings, because your dad passed peacefully," she whispered. "We just told your brother and sisters. We have been waiting for you. Where have you been?"

It was like a slap in my face from my God, from my favorite saint, and from my beloved aunt. My body froze and the tears did not make it to my eyes. Instinctively, I felt I had to hold it together for my family. I was the oldest sixteen-year-old in the whole world—at least, it felt that way for the longest time.

While I am replaying these events in my head over and over again, hoping that at some point the same movie will play differently, a gentle touch from a friend wakes me up.

"Would you like to say good-bye to your dad before the funeral?"

Earlier this morning, I had begged to see him before they took him away from me. This time, I was not going to miss the opportunity that I had foregone yesterday.

I am escorted to his side in the midst of relatives, neighbors, family friends—people I know and many I don't know. I walk gently and try to avoid their gazes by making myself invisible. Here is my daddy—a beautiful, pink-cheeked figure in his best suit. Dressed up with a tie and a big cross on his chest. There's no sign now of the awful stress caused by the bankruptcy of his business, the betrayal of his associates, the loss of his status, and the aggressive esophageal cancer that took his life in less than a year.

I move close to him, put my hands on his head. He is colder than the mountain freeze. I lean over to his ear, make sure that no one is listening, and whisper my promise to him. It is a promise that will mark my life and mark me for life. A promise that will own me, shape me, and make me who I am.

"I promise you, my beloved dad, that I will be responsible

for my mother, my brother, and my sisters. I promise you that I will fulfill your role and step into your shoes. I promise you that I will make up for your financial losses and become the successful businessperson you once were. I will continue your legacy and clean up your image for those who doubted you among your friends and family."

I close my eyes to avoid all these strangers' looks of pity and sympathy.

Uncle Joe's hand wakes me up again.

"It is time for them to take your dad to the burial site."

"Can I please come with you?" I beg.

"Absolutely not," he says. "It is against our culture. And besides, there is nothing to see."

Very disappointed, I hurriedly lean over and kiss my dad good-bye, this time overwhelmed with agony and remorse for not having done so when he was still alive.

Seven big guys appear, relatives and neighbors. They close the dark-brown coffin and carry it to nowhere. I feel like a piece of me has gone to nowhere as well.

I spent much of my life looking for that piece of me that disappeared the day of my father's funeral. Of course, I was aware of the sadness, the loss, the fear, and the intense longing that you can only feel for someone who has passed. But I was not yet aware of how my father's death truly impacted me—how the shock of that event, along with other key traumas from my childhood, caused me to construct an elaborate identity that obscured my true self from the world and from myself. It wasn't until 1994 that I began my journey into conscious awareness and began to slowly reveal this many-layered mask, which finally liberated the inner light of my true self to shine through.

How do we free ourselves from the imprints of the past and deconstruct the false identities that limit our potential for joy, creativity, and self-expression? In essence, what I learned is that we do so by becoming consciously aware—by shining the light of consciousness on emotions, beliefs, and patterns of thought and behavior that have previously been unconscious. For me, moving into conscious awareness was a journey that began with an unexpected vision in the midst of a life crisis, followed by more than two decades of intensive seeking, learning, practice, and experimentation. I will be sharing some of my story in the pages that follow, but more importantly, I will be sharing the fruits of my journey so that you can use them to transform your own life.

My intention in this book is to pay it forward to the universe. I would like to give back the treasures that I have received in my life. I would like to demystify the big principles of self-awareness and make them accessible to whoever wants to make a change in their life and create the love, peace, and joy that we all aspire to have. Some of these treasures were handed to me through grace, and some of them have been the result of my lifelong journey of discovery. After many years of spiritual work, I now have an ability to change my thought process in the moment. I wish I had been in this blessed state of awareness much earlier in my life.

These are the questions that motivated me: Would I want my kids to wait until they are my age to discover these treasures? Would they ever discover them? Would they have access to this inner joy, serenity, and happiness that I have created? Would you, the reader, have the same chance I had? Would it be possible to create a simple method to help you access this inner joy? Can I offer you a program to shift and regain this state of being anytime life events swirl you into tumultuous and murky waters? The result of this quest is the process I will be sharing in this book—a comprehensive five-stage program to transform your life through conscious awareness.

The stages are easy to remember, as they spell out the word *DANCE.*

Stage 1: **Discover Your Emotions**
Stage 2: **Awaken to Your Beliefs**

Stage 3: Name Your Patterns
Stage 4: Cancel Out Your Polarities
Stage 5: Embrace Your True Self

This five-stage process is laid out in part two of the book, and each stage is illustrated with stories from my own life experience or from people whom I personally know. (In some cases, names and details have been changed to protect identities). In addition, each step of the process includes experiential exercises to trigger your own reflection.

The exercises in this book will help you explore your inner world and expand your understanding of your emotions, your beliefs, and the patterns that govern your behavior and shape your identity. Through this process, you will be able to create and live a more authentic life. You will start letting go of what does not serve you and make space within yourself to welcome the experiences you long for—all of this and more will unfold naturally as the layers of the false self are shed. Reading this book should trigger your process of transformation, but your individual journey will be one that you alone will be creating and experiencing.

Each movement into conscious awareness is like a step in a dance. This process is not linear; it is a beautiful ballet of connections to our inner life, to self-love, and to passion. Sometimes you may feel you are stepping forward, other times, you may feel as if you are stepping back—this is all part of the dance. Each stage is a module that interconnects with the preceding and the following one, mirrors the cosmic dance of life, and connects your inner light to the universal light of consciousness.

Above all, this is a book of practice and active self-inquiry. There is great wisdom and joy to be found in ideas, and I know many people who have built upon the ideas they have learned in order to become great individuals. However, for ideas like those in this book to be transformational, it is essential that we engage with them and put them into practice. Otherwise, their effects will be short-lived, like a painkiller. We can learn new ideas in our minds but still be stuck at a deeper level of our being, repeating the broken record of our patterns throughout our lives—from one partner to another, from one job to the next, from one country to a different one—and never finding peace. Some people even use great ideas as a bypass to escape the challenges of their reality. They choose to become righteous about principles because they are not able to dive deep within and heal their basic disorder. I was one of them at one point in my life. This incited me to create practical tools that have produced a permanent, positive impact on my life.

I am writing this book for those who are like me: obstinate, resistant, impatient, and tenacious, yet determined to break through life's limitations and cause an immediate positive change in life. To you, I say: this is achievable, wherever you are on your path. Even if you are not interested in religion, spirituality, or psychology but you would like to transform your life's journey in a simple way, I hope you will find the process of this book valuable and simple to follow. Above all, I wish you all the pleasure I derive from my awakening process every time I dive in.

A final note before we dive in: for me, images are an important tool in the process of awakening, and this beautiful dance is most perfectly represented by the image of a dolphin. When I was beginning my journey, I was meditating one day, asking for guidance in a difficult decision. I waited for the answer and nothing surfaced. Just before I opened my eyes, I saw a bright-emerald crystal dolphin figurine full of light. I started laughing. What could this have to do with my dilemma? Later that day, I went to meet a friend for lunch. She apologized for being late. "While walking here, I saw something in a gift shop, something that called me in, and I felt compelled to get it for you."

A small gift box was put on my plate. Aware that the waitress was hovering impatiently, I hurried to remove the wrapping, and a small, beautiful, glass emerald dolphin appeared in front of me. To my friend's surprise, tears flooded my eyes. It was the dolphin

I had seen in my meditation. I had no idea what was going on. I thought I must be going crazy. In fact, quite the opposite was true. I was beginning my journey toward conscious awareness, and the dolphin would become a symbol for my spiritual journey.

The dolphin is a great metaphor for this work. Sometimes you may feel as if you have lost it when it disappears below the surface, only to re-appear clearly moments later. Its highly developed brain and intuition will call us to conscious awareness. Its gentle nudge will encourage us to dive deep. Its strength in riding the waves is a symbol for conquering the tribulations of our lives. Its playful flip will inspire us to change our game and not get stuck in old patterns. Its smile will remind us to have joy and gratitude. And its dance will show us how to navigate the journey with fun and grace.

What makes me most happy, what makes my heart beat faster and time fly like it does not exist, is sharing my process with others. Over the years, I have used elements of these methods to coach the leadership teams of my health centers, as well as philanthropic boards of directors, business leaders, family, and friends. Almost everyone who has applied the process has experienced a deepened awareness of at least one aspect of his or her life or business. As the work unfolded, their knowledge got deeper and richer. They were able to change their attitudes, improve their level of well-being, and find a deeper understanding of their behavior, personally or professionally. Now, through this book, in the spirit of transparency and love, I would like to share these powerful tools with you. I hope they will help you on your journey and will create the same metamorphosis in your life as they created in mine.

To you, to my children and the children of the world, I would like to give the gift of conscious awareness, so you can look at your life with a fresh pair of eyes, free from the conditioning of your past and the limitations of your thoughts. I would like to help you strip some of your experiences of their perceived significance to create the space for your true self to emerge. Throughout this voyage, we will delve into some of your past memories; uncover your stories, traumas, and convictions; and discern the beliefs that define your identity. We will identify some of your restraining patterns and isolate those emotional triggers creating dis-ease. Through the magnifying glass of conscious awareness, we will disempower these patterns, learn techniques to deal with moments of crisis, and shift from being a victim to becoming a master of our circumstances.

Once this process is completed, it will become possible for you to create and manifest the life you want for yourself. You can connect with your true self, and your own unique light will shine within you and on the people around you.

To all of my readers, I offer this prayer:

May the unknown, with its mysterious beauty, bewilder you
May the road you walk on be soft and paved with gentle experiences
May the blocks on your road be there to prevent bigger mishaps
May the storms you encounter propel you further toward your dreams
May you use the thrust of the blowing wind to learn and grow
May you flip the hurts into lessons and bounce back as quickly as you are pulled down
May you learn to heal yourself and others from the deepest of your wounds
May you become the love you live, the joy you create, and the gratitude you swim in

I am grateful to all of you, to life, to the Supreme Consciousness, to God.

PART I

AN INVITATION TO
CONSCIOUS AWARENESS

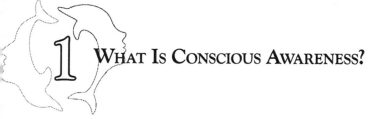

1 WHAT IS CONSCIOUS AWARENESS?

If you want to awaken all of humanity,
then awaken all of yourself.
If you want to eliminate the suffering in the world,
then eliminate all that is dark and negative in yourself.
Truly, the greatest gift you have to give
is that of your own self-transformation.
—Wang Fou, Hua Hu Chin

Have you ever uttered the words, "I didn't realize what I was doing," or "I'm not sure where that came from," after doing or saying something you later regretted? If you're an average human being, the answer is probably yes. We all, at times, find ourselves doing and saying things without knowing why, reacting in ways that surprise ourselves, and tripping over invisible obstacles in our own psyches. As human beings, we are blessed with the ability to be conscious of ourselves—to be self-aware—but for most of us, conscious awareness is not an ongoing experience. We have the capacity to observe the movements of our thoughts and feelings and make choices about whether to act on them or not. We are not blindly driven by impulse and instinct—at least, not entirely. But our degree of consciousness can vary dramatically. At times, we all feel like victims of our own unconsciousness, driven to make

1

the same mistakes over and over again by patterns and beliefs we can't even see. To liberate ourselves from this experience, we need to actively cultivate greater conscious awareness.

Conscious awareness is the state of being aware of one's own existence—one's unique thoughts, memories, feelings, sensations, surroundings, and external environment. It is a state of wakefulness of the mind.

Consciousness is an enigma. Science generally considers it to be a complex activity of the brain, but the truth is that no one has yet explained exactly where it comes from. The idea that it arises out of the brain seems implausible—if you dissect the brain, you cannot see consciousness, just as you cannot see thoughts or beliefs. I like to think of the brain as its conduit. We need the brain to process consciousness.

Spiritual teachers and thinkers are less concerned with where consciousness comes from; in fact, many of them believe that everything comes from it. Deepak Chopra, in *The Seven Spiritual Laws of Success,* writes: "The source of all creation is pure consciousness … pure potentiality seeking expression from the unmanifest to the manifest. And when we realize that our true Self is one of pure potentiality we align with the power that manifests everything in the universe."[1]

Like Chopra, I see consciousness as being both a human faculty and a divine state of being. In the human sense, consciousness is our awareness, cognition, perceptions, beliefs, emotions, and so on; in the divine sense, it is a field of infinite possibilities and potentiality. Divine or higher consciousness is the origin of everything, and therefore, it is also the nature of our true selves.

The premise of this book is that when we align our human consciousness to higher consciousness, we become consciously aware beings, connected to our true selves. We come closer to understanding the relationship between our human nature and our spiritual nature, and we become able to integrate them in a meaningful way. When we are not trapped in the limiting beliefs of the past, we can start pulling any possibility of what we want to become from the field of the unmanifest.

In this book, I have created a process that can clear your thoughts, beliefs, emotions, and patterns to allow you to connect to divine consciousness, the universal light. There are many terms in the spiritual and religious traditions for this ultimate dimension. You can use the term *God* if you are comfortable with it. Or you may prefer: *Supreme Intelligence, Great Spirit, Creator, Higher Power, the One*, or any other name that represents that all-encompassing light. I like to use several of these terms interchangeably, but I often choose the *Source*, as it points to this dimension as the origin of everything.

Conscious awareness is not something that we get. It is something we unearth within ourselves. Within all of us, there is an awareness that is still and conscious at all times. It is that awareness that we need to connect to the Source or higher consciousness. Conscious awareness is a dance with the universe—a dance between self-awareness and a conscious recognition of our union with the Source.

The problem, for most of us, is that we are disconnected from our true selves. We have built up layer upon layer of a false identity, based on our conditioning, our beliefs, and our traumatic experiences. To put it simply, this constructed identity is what spiritual teachers refer to as the *ego*, although there are many different ways this term is used in academic psychology. For the purposes of this book, I define *ego* as the constructed identity that obscures the true self. Contemporary author Eckhart Tolle refers to the ego as the illusory self, because it embodies a misperception of who we are. He writes: "Ego is always identification with form, seeking yourself and thereby losing yourself in some form. Forms are not just material objects and physical bodies. More fundamental than the external forms—things and bodies—are the thought forms that continuously arise in the field of consciousness."[2]

Most of our frustrations stem from the fact that we believe

something is wrong inside and needs to be fixed; in reality, nothing needs to be fixed, only uncovered. It all begins with self-awareness. My intention for you is that each day, as you complete the chapters and do the work, your awareness will expand and will awaken to the origin of your true nature. Each day, through your readings and the stillness of the moment, you will learn how to connect deeply to your true self. I hope that you will feel joy, passion, and abundant love as you reconnect with your natural state of conscious awareness. Over time, you'll be able to create a magical relationship with yourself and with each person who crosses your path.

Many of the great spiritual teachers and wise men and women throughout the ages have spoken of conscious awareness or self-awareness as the highest form of human attainment. Spiritual seekers have answered the call to "know thyself" by journeying within in search of enlightenment. Psychologists, too, have helped us to shed light on the inner workings of our minds and emotions and bring them into awareness.

I like to think of conscious awareness as a process, not an attainment. It is a journey with no end point, for there is always more to uncover. For the sake of this work, I define conscious awareness as a process by which the subconscious or unconscious becomes intentionally conscious. (For the purposes of this book, I am not distinguishing between the subconscious and the unconscious, although psychologists use these terms in different ways.) Conscious awareness is the process of purposefully observing and distinguishing your patterns at play, their connection with your actions and reactions, and their impact on others and yourself. You become deliberately aware of what operates your life by opening yourself up to yourself, to others, and to the Source with love and compassion.

Conscious awareness can allow you to master your circumstances and drive your life, rather than being influenced by your past or held back by your limiting beliefs. It will help you choose your responses based on the clarity of the facts and become cognizant of what is at play in your life moment by moment.

Jungian psychology uses the term *individuation* to describe the process of transforming one's psyche by bringing the personal and collective unconscious into conscious. If I were to draw a parallel, I would say that the process of conscious awareness is a process of individuation. It has a comprehensive healing and transformative effect on the person, mentally, physically, and spiritually.

In Sigmund Freud's theory of personality, the conscious mind consists of everything inside of our awareness, but much of what occurs within and between us is subconscious. Freud used the metaphor of the physical makeup of an iceberg to describe these two major aspects of human personality. The tip of the iceberg that extends above the water represents the conscious mind, while the vast mass below the surface is the subconscious. Our subconscious behavior is a result of social and cultural programming that has often taken place decades, centuries, or millennia ago and therefore limits and inhibits us from being more effective.

It is widely accepted by psychologists, from Freud and Jung to more modern scholars, that by the time human beings are around seven years of age, ninety percent of all the learning and habits in our life have been formed and become subconscious. We have formed the habits of walking, talking, and thinking and have developed coping survival mechanisms. We have also established our beliefs around things like success and relationships and have inherited inner programming and thinking patterns that may be either positive or toxic in nature.

Since the twentieth century, much has been written about the conscious and the subconscious or unconscious mind. In modern cognitive psychology, many researchers have emphasized the degree to which cognitive processing happens outside the scope of cognitive awareness.

This book does not specifically address the psychological or neurological aspects of the mind. Rather, it focuses on offering practical ways to find clues as to how to access some of the toxic subconscious patterns we have and to transform and transcend them through a conscious awareness process. The compelling question behind this work is: What if the mental programming that you currently have within you is stopping you from achieving your dreams, goals, and desires? How can you move past the inner voices that have kept you where you are?

To change is never a comfortable act—especially at the level of consciousness. It entails overcoming our natural tendencies, our conditioning, and our hereditary programming in order to adapt to a new reality. Let's be honest here: Who among us likes to change and relinquish the old, when it has become comfortable and easy? We often say, "If it's not broken, why fix it?" Letting go of the old patterns and embracing the new and unknown is not a simple task. That is why most of us will only decide to pick up a book like this when our lives start being uncomfortable, when things get so bad that we can no longer afford not to make a change. Those who are able to be pro-active in these matters, inspired by an inner knowing and a desire to lead the way for others, are few. But whether the challenges in your life have pushed you to transform or you are among those rare proactive individuals, you are one of the pioneers of higher consciousness. Those individuals who choose to become more consciously aware will alter the pathways of their emotional and psychological patterns. And that's not all; some scientists now tell us we may even be able to cause a change on a genetic level.

While still in its infancy, the new science of epigenetics is revealing that our genes are influenced by many more factors than scientists had ever considered before. Developmental biologist Bruce Lipton, in his book *The Biology of Belief*, writes:

> *Epigenetics*, which literally means "control over genes," has completely upended our conventional understanding of genetic control. Epigenetics is the science of how environmental signals select, modify, and regulate gene activity. This new awareness reveals that the activity of our genes

is constantly being modified in response to life experiences. Which again emphasizes that our perceptions of life shape our biology.[3]

What this means for us is that by affecting our beliefs, emotional states, and behavioral patterns and by healing our negative traumas, we may be able to influence our genes. And in so doing, we will transform not just our own lives but also the legacy we pass on to our children, grandchildren, and our evolving species. This, in a nutshell, is the rationale behind the process of conscious awareness described in this book. Self-discovery requires commitment, courage, and perseverance. Furthermore, it requires the inner conviction that it matters, not just for individuals but also for humanity. Imagine being part of a world where most people around you—you included—are well adapted and at peace.

Life is a constantly evolving process. I believe that the purpose of our human experience is to awaken who we truly are and connect back to higher consciousness. Through the process of our own healing, we help heal others and the planet. When we are on the path of conscious awareness, we are contributing to the flow of conscious evolution. To consciously participate in the evolutionary process, you have to keep flowing with it. Imagine that you are a dolphin swimming freely with the currents of life, rather than a rock that obstructs the flow.

This evolutionary process is not linear. As we go through experiences and challenges in our lives, our conscious awareness unfolds in leaps and bounds. We fall, we learn, we get up, we develop our game, and we move forward with the evolutionary process. If we resist, shut down, hold a grudge, engage in violence, or become bitter from our experiences, we become like the hard rock in the middle of the stream. We block ourselves from evolving and do not contribute to the whole.

The process of conscious awareness is not an easy one. It can be confronting and disconcerting at times. But if you continue to stick with it, you will transform your views, and your perceptions may lead you even beyond your intended outcome. On this path, every challenge becomes a teacher and every trauma provides an opening for a leap in consciousness. Every difficult person in our lives becomes an assignment for growth and development and gives us the chance to practice these principles. Every sickness becomes our spiritual master. The lessons that we don't learn will keep showing up in our lives until we learn them. The bigger the challenge, the bigger the opportunity becomes for conscious evolution and healing. When approached in this way, the process of conscious awareness becomes a continuous dance with the movement of life.

2 PLANNING YOUR JOURNEY

A goal without a plan is just a wish.
—Antoine de Saint-Exupéry

When you are embarking on an important journey—perhaps the journey of a lifetime—it's important to take time to plan and prepare. You would not set out to travel through an unknown country without considering your route, planning ahead, learning about the places you could visit and the things you could discover, packing what you would need for the journey, and ensuring you are equipped to navigate the terrain ahead. The same rule applies when your journey takes you through the inner landscapes of consciousness. Preparation is essential. Before we dive in, here are some suggestions about how you can prepare yourself to get the most benefit from the process. Following these guidelines will help to ensure that the time and energy you put into the practice will be rewarded with transformation.

SET YOUR INTENTION

It is essential to set an intention for your process toward conscious awareness. Although it is a journey and not a destination, it is important to know what you are longing for in life. It is like setting

9

a direction in your GPS. When you set an intention, you create an attractor that can pull you toward it. As spiritual teachers often say, "Where attention goes, energy flows." Setting a clear intention redirects your attention, which opens up a channel for energy to be directed toward achieving that intention. Your actions are direct responses to your beliefs, and your beliefs are patterns of thoughts. Your beliefs direct your feelings, and your feelings are a magnet of focused energy that can create what you want in your life. So if you set an intention and you believe in it, your actions will be aligned with that which brings you closer to your intention.

When you think about your intention, ask yourself what you would like to achieve for you and your life through the process. Your intention should always be about yourself, never about someone else. Write down your intention for yourself and read it every day. Ask yourself the question: What would it be like for me if my intention materializes? Visualize yourself and your life when your intention is fulfilled. Feel the emotion that the fulfillment of this goal will bring to you. Connect with this feeling every time you think about it. It is like planting a seed—you will nurture it every time you think about it. Setting an intention for your process will allow you to measure your progress and the success of this process in a tangible, meaningful way.

Your intention should be positive; for example, if your intention is to get rid of fear in your life, set your intention as: *my intention is to have courage in my life*. It is preferable to use the present tense and avoid the words *would* and *should*. Although you can be as specific as you want in setting an intention, the nature of this work has to do with conscious awareness; therefore, I recommend that your intention-setting be focused on the domain of consciousness. Think of your intentions in terms of the states of being that you want to attain, rather than specific achievements like getting a new job or getting married. Of course, getting a new job or getting married may occur as a by-product of your state of being or as a result of your conscious awareness, but this process focuses on creating the shift in consciousness first. It's important that while you believe and feel your intention, you let go of attachment to a specific form that the outcome should take. When you shift your state of being, you open yourself up to possibilities you may not have imagined yet.

Although intentions point us toward the future, using the present tense instead of the future tense helps you set your intentions in motion right now. For example, "I am loving" instead of "I intend to create love in my life." Your intention becomes an affirmation. Here are some more examples:

- I am being peaceful.
- I am making a contribution to the lives of others.
- I am living a life of integrity.
- I am living in abundance.
- I am being joyful in my life.
- I am forgiving "so and so."
- I am forgiving myself.
- I am loving myself.
- I am connecting with my purpose.
- I am being self-expressed in my life.

CULTIVATE AN OPEN MINDSET AND A CLEAR-EYED VIEW

If you want to derive the maximum benefit from this process, it is important to allow what is present in your subconscious to surface, without interference. If arbitrated, what is there will not show up. Therefore, when embarking on this journey, I would like to urge you to create the right mindset for the process. In order to allow what is there to reveal itself, you will need to suspend all judgment toward yourself and others. I find that this is very challenging for most people, and for some people more than others.

Creating an open mind and an open heart is important mental preparation for doing this work. While diving deep, you will be reliving some difficult experiences and visiting some touchy areas of your past. Please relinquish any fears, worries, or doubts you may have and remain open to the experience without judgment. The resurgence of old, painful memories associated with previous events is inevitable. You may get in touch with feelings of anger, grief, or sadness embodied in your memories. While you are allowing these events and emotions to resurface, they should not be a target for your judgment and criticism.

I would like to invite you to become acquainted with the concept of the "clear-eyed view." A clear eye, for the purpose of this work, will be defined as an eye that simply sees what is. There is no right or wrong for the clear eye. There is what there is, and it is what it is. The clear eye sees only the facts. A clear-eyed view lets everything be the way it is without suppressing it, editing it, or judging it. It is a pure snapshot of events taken without a filter. It is basic observation free from any assessment.

Here's a simple technique to help facilitate a clear-eyed view: try to be the observer of what is happening in your life rather than just the actor—the "eye of the I," as spiritual teachers sometimes call it. Every time you catch yourself judging others and yourself, simply say the words: *allow and let it be.*

Creating this mindset involves opening your heart to your own life and its makeup, and it will help you open your heart to other people's lives and experiences. The key to peace is not only being peaceful with where you are but also be peaceful with where others are. A clear-eyed view will enhance the objectivity of our life stories as we relate them; it will reduce our life's drama and help us focus and direct our life's game based on what really matters.

Set Aside Time and Space for Your Work

It is important to find a specific time of the day that you will choose to do your transformational work, allocating at least a half hour per exercise. This will help you to establish a routine of going within, even after the method is completed.

What is the right time? Any time you look forward to doing your process is the right time. Mornings and evenings coincide with our body's quieter rhythms, so many people find these times particularly conducive. The risk, however, is that you may be more likely to fall asleep while doing the exercises at these times. If this happens, it is only normal, and you can set aside a time during your day to start over again.

Setting aside as little as thirty minutes each day to read a chapter and do an exercise will start creating the intended result incrementally, even after you finish reading the book. The process will continue to unfold day by day after each self-discovery.

You may also want to consider setting up a peaceful, comfortable place for your daily practice. Creating your sacred space—whether it is at home, in your office, or somewhere in nature—is an important way to support your work. Your spot must be private, safe, and quiet, with minimal distractions.

ALLOW YOURSELF AS LONG AS YOU NEED TO COMPLETE THE PROCESS

The time that is needed for reading this book and completing the exercises will be totally different from one person to the next. We move at different paces in our lives. How long it takes you will depend on the time you allocate to reading this book and doing the exercises. It will also depend on your life process and whether you have been previously exposed to any deep introspective work in the past. Some chapters include only one exercise, while some include several. Don't rush through them; give each exercise the time and space it needs, even if it takes you several days to work through each chapter. And if you feel you need to, I recommend that you go back to each chapter and redo the exercises as many times as you feel is necessary before you move to the next section. You can even go back to earlier chapters and do the exercises again at any time while reading this book.

Our life events have built up many layers of stories and conditioning inside us. As you progress in reading this book and completing your exercises, you may find that you suddenly become aware of another, deeper layer that you need to attend to. I urge you to let your spontaneity direct you to where you need to be and trust that this will be the right place for you. However, following the sequence of the chapters is important to maximize the effect of this book. Do the exercises for the first time in the order presented, and then go back and repeat if needed.

DEDICATE A NOTEBOOK

Purchase and keep a notebook or journal. This will be your memoir. It will be an interesting piece of work that you can keep with your personal cherished items. It is a diary with a purpose; it will show your progress but mostly will be the expression of your conscious awareness. I encourage you to document every time you do your exercises and also any insights you have in between. Some of you will discard your notebooks after finishing the process, and some will share them for others to get inspired or even publish them. Who knows? But for the purpose of this work, it is a private journal for your eyes only. You can visit my website at www.TheDolphinsDance.com to download a specially designed workbook that includes all the exercises we will be doing in this book.

A NOTE ABOUT THE EXERCISES

Each chapter in this book includes at least one exercise; some include several. Each exercise builds on what has come before, so you will be repeating some steps at the beginning of each one. Many of the exercises are designed around asking yourself questions and allowing the answers to arise within a state of relaxation.

You can do these exercises alone, or you may also choose to do them with a trusted partner. If you work with a partner, you can have him or her ask you the questions instead of asking them to yourself. In this case, I would recommend that you decide before beginning which of you will be the subject of the exercise and which is the questioner. Don't move back and forth. Complete the exercise before switching places.

Here are a few general instructions for approaching the exercises:

- It is important to be in a state of relaxation before you begin asking the questions. I will be teaching you a process to achieve this in the next chapter.
- Sometimes, each step includes several questions. You may need to read these several times, but then close your eyes to allow the answer to arise before opening your eyes and writing it down.
- When you ask yourself a question, choose the first answer that comes to your mind. Don't spend too much time thinking about the questions or trying to figure out the answers. When an answer arises, sit quietly with it for a moment, and then write it down in your notebook.
- Pause between questions. If an answer does not come to you, leave that question open and give it time and space to unfold on its own. You can always come back and write it down when it does.
- The answers need not to be interpreted, just uncovered. At times you may notice that there is a common theme to your answers that will lead you to what you are trying to unearth.
- There are no right or wrong answers; allow whatever arises to just be, without judging it.

With these preparations in place, we are almost ready to begin our journey into conscious awareness. However, there is one final piece of preparation we must undertake. Before we can journey through the landscape of consciousness, we must learn how to access the space within. In the next chapter, I'll be teaching you a method for accessing your inner space and clearing out the clutter that often obscures it. This simple but powerful method will become foundational to all the exercises I'll be sharing later in this book, so let's take a moment now to learn how to dive into deep inner space.

3 Accessing the Space Within

Go inwards. Find your inner space, and suddenly, you
will find an explosion of light, of beauty, of ecstasy—
as if suddenly thousands of roses have blossomed
within you and you are full of their fragrance.
—Osho

I still vividly remember the first time I discovered the infinite space within myself. The words came out of my mouth unexpectedly during a transformational workshop:

"I am nothing. I am only a space through which things happen."

Angelo, the workshop leader, asked me to repeat it. "It is music to my ears," he declared. I said it again. "I am really nothing; I am only a space through which things happen."

Every time I echoed the phrase, I felt lighter and lighter. When I stopped restating it, Angelo asked us all to pause and take a break. During the break, many fellow participants came up to me and told me that something had shifted for them as I was repeating the words, even if they did not fully get the meaning. One participant said that he saw light in the room. Another felt chills. A beautiful old lady realized that whatever she was holding onto became nothing.

It was a true "aha" moment for me, early in my transformational process. The insight I had that day continues to be foundational to my work: who and what we really are is empty space. As we have discussed in the previous chapter, our true nature is pure consciousness. Consciousness is not a thing; it is a space, within which things like thoughts, feelings, and beliefs arise.

Everything that occurs in the universe has a space allocated for it. We exist as a function of space. When we come to this earth, we are granted a space that we occupy on a physical, psychological, mental, vibrational, metaphysical, etheric, and energetic level. It is a visible and invisible space. Our consciousness occupies a space that is invisible to us. The gift of life is a gift of space.

The empty space between thoughts—that interval of time where the mind goes blank—is the space that connects us to who we are, to our true nature, to the deep feeling of oneness with everything, to God. But as the ancient philosopher Aristotle said, "Nature abhors a vacuum." Nature requires every space to be filled with something. The same principle applies to us. As soon as we feel the emptiness, we try to fill it with our thoughts, opinions, and conditioning. We crowd the space with our fears of not being good enough or lovable enough, our ideas on how to self-improve, our "shoulds" and "shouldn'ts." At times, we try to fill our space with food, addictions, and distractions. How do we hold an inner open space against all odds? Is there a way for love and connection to emerge in this space instead of all the mumbo jumbo that we tend to hold within us?

The process of conscious awareness is about clearing the inner space to make room for your real self to emerge. When I refer to "clearing the space," I mean releasing the emotions that are holding thoughts, patterns, and blocks. I will be showing you how to do this in the chapters to come. Basically, we need to access the deep space within and awaken to what inhabits it—the beliefs and patterns that control our psychological and emotional states of being, which generate our actions and expressions in the world. We need to clear the space within, much like the process of removing the weeds prior to planting a garden in order to allow the good plants to blossom. The junk certainly does not serve us anymore, but it occupies a space nonetheless, which prevents our true selves from showing up.

Another way to understand the process of conscious awareness is that it is about decreasing the space between you and the Source and increasing the space between you and your thoughts. When you can create a space between you and your thoughts, between you and your emotions, between you and your beliefs, between you and what you do, between you and what you have, between you and your core patterns, between you and your shadows, you become the observer of all the above and you start dissociating yourself from all of it. It becomes more difficult for you to identify with your thoughts, your emotions, your beliefs, your possessions, your core patterns, and your shadows. And simultaneously, when you reduce the space between you and the Source, you get closer to the Source. When you eliminate the space between you and the Source, you can identify with it, merge with it, and become it.

By achieving conscious awareness, we become a space for the Source to manifest through us. We can't become a space for the Source if who we are as a space is filled with false beliefs and limiting patterns. Once we become aware of these beliefs and patterns, we start disempowering them. In doing so, we clear the space and allow true consciousness to flow through us. We become a conduit for it as whatever was cluttering the space dissipates.

First, however, we need to learn to access the space itself. This will be the foundation of all the exercises in this book; it is where we will start each time. We need to access the deep space within us and be aware of its occupants, because what is within us manifests itself outside of us. Quieting the mind and stopping the agitation within is an essential component for this access. The ancient practice of meditation, along with deep relaxation, hypnosis, self-hypnosis, subliminal mind work, and dream work, is a vehicle by which we can access the subconscious.

Meditators from the East and the West, among many traditions, agree as to the relevance of meditation practice in the process of awareness. It was even referred to in the scriptures as the presence of God. The prophet Elijah found God not in the wind, the earthquake, or the fire, but in "the sound of silence" (1 Kings 19:11, 12). Silence and stillness are a means to connect to your true self and give you access to the higher power outside of you.

Because conscious awareness is a process by which the subconscious or unconscious becomes intentionally conscious, I propose that accessing the deep inner space will help us access our subconscious mind with time.

EXERCISE 1: CREATE YOUR SAFE SPACE: THE CLEAR LAGOON

The prerequisite for all of the exercises in this book is a state of relaxation; therefore, it is of the utmost importance to learn how to do this effectively. Even if you do not have time to do the exercises every day, I recommend that you practice accessing a state of relaxation or meditation daily—as little as five minutes can make a difference. It will become a safe haven you can retreat to when you need a break from all the hustle and bustle of your daily activities or if you are looking for an answer to a question. Through stillness, you can access what is unconscious and bring it to the surface. You can watch your mind with detachment and open and deepen your observation. You can make your state of relaxation a daily practice in the morning when you wake up, in the evening before you go to bed, or anytime during your day. (See Appendix 1, p. 169, for some suggested daily meditation formats.)

In accessing this state of relaxation, it is helpful to visually create a mental space, a place of stillness. Through visualizing a peaceful scene, you can activate your imagination to create a state of deep relaxation. Imagine a place of beauty where your senses are totally immersed in splendor and silence. With time and practice, visualizing this space while breathing will help you access your inner space more quickly and deeply. The image I use is a place I call the "Clear Lagoon." It is a place of clarity, quiet, and depth. I will share the images I use, but your Clear Lagoon is your own creation, and you should adapt it in whatever way feels right for you. It is a mind tool to help you access stillness quicker.

I will teach you this exercise in detail now, as it will become the first step of all the future exercises in the book. In order not to repeat the instructions, in later chapters, I will simply ask you to return to your Clear Lagoon.

I suggest that you read the instructions all the way through and then practice the exercise. You can repeat it as many times as you like during your day. You will notice an instant relaxation and mental clarity after you do. Ready? Let's dive in.

Step 1

Choose a private place where you can sit in silence without interruption for about half an hour.

Step 2

Find a way to sit that is comfortable and relaxed. It is preferable to sit up straight, but you can choose to sit on the floor, on a cushion, or on a chair. If you like to lie down, that is fine too. Uncross your hands and relax them in your lap, palms up or down.

Step 3

While sitting in silence, suspend all judgment about yourself, your thoughts, and the people in your life. Just observe, and don't judge what is surfacing. If you get emotional, let it be, and don't engage your mind in any criticism, assessment, or decision-making. Just observe and focus on your breathing.

Thoughts will inevitably rush through your mind—that's normal. Don't try to do anything with them; just let them be, and try to allow whatever comes up to surface. The key to accessing this space within is to quiet your mind, to observe the noise without resistance and turn the volume down. The thoughts may not disappear, but you will experience that there is more space and lag time between you and them. Try to be present with your inner self without judgment.

STEP 4

While sitting comfortably, take three deep breaths. Inhale to the count of four; hold your breath to the count of two; exhale to the count of four. Relax. This will create the intended relaxation in the present moment. Now, close your eyes. Repeat the breathing exercise three times, this time inhaling to the count of six, holding your breath to the count of three, and exhaling to the count of six. Notice how you become more relaxed with each breath. Inhale calmness, and exhale all the tension of your day. Notice how you become lighter with each breath. Breathe slowly and deeply while paying attention to your breath. Count slowly from ten to one. After the counting, allow your breath to flow in and out effortlessly for few minutes in an unforced, natural rhythm.

STEP 5

Continue breathing deeply. Now, picture a ball of white light descending from your head to all parts of your body. Allow yourself to visualize its brightness and to feel its warmth. Starting from your head, relax every muscle in your body, from your facial muscles to your neck, down to your shoulders, and so on. As the light descends through your body, it caresses your organs gently and stops where it feels pain and discomfort. It stays there until the feeling of ease in the organ comes back. It continues descending though the body until it reaches the lower extremities. All tension starts to disappear. I usually start by visualizing the light as white, but as it moves through my body, it starts taking on different shapes and colors. You may experience a tingling sensation or a throbbing in certain areas of your body. This is normal. When you begin to relax deeply, your body may feel warmer. You are in complete harmony with the light.

STEP 6

Now, imagine yourself sitting alone under a palm tree in front of a beautiful, calm lagoon. Picture the blue sky above you; see the light reflecting in the still, clear water; listen to the song of the birds; feel the gentle breeze. On the surface of the water, there are white swans and an intelligent dolphin that dives deep and from time to time jumps and flips with total ease and happiness. Imagine the flowers and the colors that you love around the Lagoon, and notice a big, beautiful lotus flower close to the bank. Imagine an animal that you love quietly resting on the grass. Soak in all this beauty and hold it inside yourself, and then breathe out again.

Beside the Lagoon, you can feel safe and secure. The water has a cleansing effect and can regenerate though its beauty and purity. Remember the scene and the feeling it evokes in you. You can carry this image with you wherever you go. Once you have invented this place, you simply need to recall this visual scene any time you need to access a place of peace where you can relax and feel safe. You will be using this place as the starting point for each of the exercises in this book.

STEP 7

When you are ready, breathe deeply and count from one to ten, and then open your eyes.

STEP 8

You may want to take your notebook and write a description of your Clear Lagoon, adding as much sensory detail as you can. Describe how it looks and how you feel when you are sitting there.

PART II

THE DOLPHIN'S DANCE:
A FIVE-STAGE PROCESS

4 STAGE 1: DISCOVER YOUR EMOTIONS

*It takes courage … to endure the sharp pains of self
discovery rather than choose to take the dull pain of
unconsciousness that would last the rest of our lives.*
—Marianne Williamson, *A Return to Love:
Reflections on the Principles of "A Course in Miracles"*

Through the Dolphin's DANCE process, we will be uncovering
what I call your Identity Signature, which is the unique and
complex matrix of emotions, beliefs, and behavior patterns that
you have constructed over the course of your lifetime. This Identity
Signature is what obscures your true self, and through bringing it
into conscious awareness, you will be able to rediscover who you
really are and allow your light to shine into the world, unobstructed.

There are three components to your Identity Signature: I call these
your Emotional Logo, your Belief Matrix, and your Behavior Patterns.
In each of the first three stages of the DANCE, we will uncover one
of these components and slowly fill out the picture by adding the key
elements one by one. Don't worry if it sounds complex—we humans
are complex creatures, and in order to become consciously aware, it is
important to honor and respect this truth. This process is structured
in such a way that you can move slowly, step by step, into a deeper
understanding of the unique constructs of your own inner space.

The first stage focuses on discovering the emotions that are at the root of who you are and how you show up in the world. By "how you show up," I mean how you think, what you believe, and how you behave. Each of us has what I call an Emotional Logo—a pattern of emotions and reactions that are like a unique personal trademark, created out of particular events in our lives. This is the first part of your Identity Signature. To understand your particular Emotional Logo, you will be guided to identify its three key elements:

> **Your Marker**—a painful and traumatic event that happened in your early life and marked you forever, which shaped your behavior whether or not you are aware of it.

> **Your Sticker**—the traumatic emotion that resurges every time a threat of an event similar in nature to the Marker occurs in your life.

> **Your Vessel**—the part of your body where your Sticker resides and is felt as a physical sensation.

It is interesting to me that the word *emotion* stems from the Latin *emovere*, which means, "move out, remove, or agitate." Emotions do indeed agitate lifetimes of feelings, reactions, and beliefs. They are deeply bound up with the issues we struggle with, the patterns we find ourselves trapped in, and the pain we continue to suffer. In this first stage, we will be using these powerful emotions as a doorway to dive deep and uncover the roots of our negative beliefs about ourselves, which drive so much of our suffering.

This step of the DANCE is a basic one because it provides easy access to the subconscious through following your emotions. However, while it may be an easy point of entry, it may at the same time stir up some deeply buried emotions within. As you go through this stage, remember that this is a stepping-stone to transforming your negative belief and reestablishing a connection with your inner self.

EMOTIONS, FEELINGS, AND SENSATIONS: UNDERSTANDING THE DIFFERENCE

The method I will be sharing in this section is designed to help you open up and access your state of being by recognizing your emotions. Opening up to your emotions will allow space for your real self to come forward authentically into the world. In order to understand the reasons why we experience life in the ways that we do, it's important to uncover and observe our emotional makeup with an unbiased eye. If we want to free ourselves from the recurring emotional responses that keep playing out in our lives and the reactions they drive, we have to take a look at their early expressions and liberate them from being tied to the first traumatic incidents in our lives, so they can surface without any judgment or limitation. In other words, the purpose of this chapter is to allow us to become consciously aware of our emotional selves. It is only a conscious mind that has the capacity to question our reactions and transform them into focused actions. First, however, we need to make a distinction between emotions, feelings, and sensations. We are accustomed to using the terms *emotion, feeling,* and *sensation* interchangeably, but they, in fact, have different meanings, which can help us to see our experience more clearly. Here are some simple distinctions that will help clarify how I am using these terms. Let's start with *feeling* and *emotion.*

Emotions are physiological experiences that are triggered by internal or external events. Emotions are somatic, meaning, literally, they are "of the body." We may not be conscious of them while they are arising, but they can be objectively measured by physical factors like blood flow, brain activity, and facial expressions.

Feelings are secondary. They live in our minds and represent our subjective experience of our emotions after they have occurred, the meanings we give to them, and the language we use to describe them.

Feelings are our impressions and interpretations of our emotions. Antonio R. Damasio, MD, a neuroscientist at USC, explains:

> Emotions are more or less the complex reactions the body has to certain stimuli. When we are afraid of something, our hearts begin to race, our mouths become dry, our skin turns pale and our muscles contract. This emotional reaction occurs automatically and unconsciously. Feelings occur after we become aware in our brain of such physical changes; only then do we experience the feeling of fear.[4]

Karla McLaren, author of *The Art of Empathy,* sums up this distinction simply: "An *emotion* is a physiological experience (or state of awareness) that gives you information about the world, and a *feeling* is your conscious awareness of the emotion itself."[5]

McLaren points out that some people have difficulty connecting feelings to emotions due to their lack of awareness of their emotions. They may feel fearful, but underneath, in fact, they are angry. It is only when someone points out to them that they are behaving strangely or names their emotion, or they drop into a severe depression or crisis, that they start becoming aware of it.

Now that we've made these distinctions, what we will try to unearth are the emotions that arose from an initial traumatic experience in your life, which I call the Marker. These are the emotions that can be triggered by similar events or by thoughts evoking similar events.

Uncover Your Marker

Distinguishing the traumatic events that marked us is an essential step in the process of self-discovery. You may have forgotten some events that occurred when you were very young, yet their impact is still playing a significant role in how you live your life today. It is like a low-volume instrument playing in the background of your being. No matter what you do, the instrument plays; you can't shut it off. When you try to sleep, it is there. When you wake up, it is still there. When you communicate with people, it is playing. You get so accustomed to it that you are not even aware of its sound.

Some traumas are so painful that we do not even want to remember them. Some are suppressed from our consciousness, even if we were old enough to recall them. We may be selectively amnesic toward some occurrences because we could not handle the pain they generated. Yet if these events are not brought to the surface, we won't be able to relate to ourselves with the intimacy for which we are longing. We will use our crisis as a starting point on our journey—a place to temporarily anchor ourselves and then begin to navigate forward.

It is very important to go back in time to your early childhood age and uncover the most painful events of your life. These events are indicators that can help us to decipher the patterns in our lives. They are associated with intense emotions, feelings, and sensations. They made you form certain opinions about yourself (usually variations on "something is not right" or "I am not okay."). These thoughts got stored in your subconscious mind and affected your actions and reactions in the world without your knowledge.

Your Marker event is at the source of your ailments, your frustration, and your feeling that something needs to be fixed. It could be a loss or abandonment. It could be an incident that gave rise to deep embarrassment or shame. It could be verbal or physical abuse. Whatever it was, it triggered an emotion and a feeling that stuck with you. You may want to forget about these events, but your subconscious mind has stored them and kept them active without your conscious permission. The emotions, sensations, and feelings that initially accompanied these childhood events are still acting up and causing your reactions. Don't you wonder why you find some experiences in your life particularly painful to you, although they may seem minor and insignificant to other people? For example, if your traumatic incident had to do with loss, you are likely to react more acutely to even minor losses in your life than others do.

Becoming aware of your Marker will help you release the emotion and the unhealthy belief about yourself that you carry with you wherever you are and wherever you go. Therefore, the starting point of this process is to dive in and become aware of your painful stories and all of the meanings, emotions, feelings, and sensations associated with them. Some of you may find this first stage intense—we will be accompanying our friendly dolphin into deep and murky waters. But please stay with me and give it a try. If you persevere beyond these early phases, the work will gradually become lighter and the clarity you will gain about your life will make you enjoy the experience and look forward to more of it.

So how do we get in touch with these Marker events and make them resurface despite the discomfort that this may create? How do we unearth them from our unconsciousness? I recommend that you go back as far as you can into your childhood memories. Sometimes, the original incident behind your emotional makeup may not be immediately obvious, but if you start with the first one that comes to you, it may lead you back to others.

In order to nudge you into diving deep within, I will share my own Marker events. As you read mine, keep thinking of your own. I will share these with you in the way that they came to me—two key events linked to the same emotions. I started being aware of the one that I remembered most easily, which was the loss of my dad at age sixteen—the story I shared with you in the opening pages of this book. This led me back to the earlier, underlying event, which happened when I was about ten, and which I will share with you now. You will notice that I write about this event in quite a lot of detail, in the present tense as I try to put myself back in the scene and express it in such a way that conveys the immediacy of the experience—the feelings, thoughts, images, sounds, and sensations.

When we go through the exercise to retrieve your Marker event, I encourage you to write it down in a similar style.

MY MARKER

I hear my father cry as I am standing by his bedroom door. I can feel his pain and sense his fear. I am about ten years old. It has been a normal day at school, and life is good. I finished my homework before dinner, and our nanny is about to turn on the black-and-white TV. We are allowed to watch TV for half an hour before supper if we have finished our homework. But something is wrong this evening. When Dad came home, his face was sad, and he did not kiss me as he usually does but instead called my mom to the room and shut the door. I can hear his muffled voice.

"We are finished; we lost everything. There is nobody out there who can help us. We have a lot of receivables out with people that we will recover after the syndic collects them. But for now, I'm sorry. I tried everything I could, but we declared bankruptcy today."

My mom is sobbing. He's telling her they will confiscate our car, a beautiful, sporty Camaro that he loves. They will seize our house shortly after. Who are these villains who will be appropriating our belongings? Are they witches, monsters, or criminals? Who is the syndic who may help us out? Is he a hero? An angel? A superman? I am worried for my parents, but part of me is excited about meeting the villains and the hero and getting to side with the brave men.

And then my mom asks, "What will happen to Aya?" Our nanny.

"We have to let her go," my father replies. "I called her father today, and he will pick her up tomorrow. I'm so sorry. We are ruined. It's all over."

Enough with the fairytale villains and heroes—what do they mean, Aya is leaving? I can't possibly live without her. She takes care of my siblings and me. I love her. Who else will be my friend?

I don't want to lose our house and the stupid Camaro that gets more attention than I do. I run into the bathroom and stay there.

Later, Aya and I cry together while I watch her pack. I desperately try to figure out a way to stop her from leaving but I fail. In the days that follow, nothing is the same. The rug is literally being pulled from under our feet. Our home is full of movers, packers, men wearing black suits with papers and folders counting our furniture. They even go through my room, opening drawers and closets. My piggy bank, my bear, and my favorite doll all disappear.

A few weeks later, we move to a small, two-bedroom apartment in a different building. Slowly, some feelings of normalcy return. I hear our story being repeated to our new neighbors, new friends, and family so many times. It starts to feel familiar to me. I survived. Then one day, I hear another serious conversation between my parents. My dad tells my mom that he got a job in Kuwait City, where he will make enough money for us until the syndic collects ours.

"We will cover our debt and recoup our house up in the mountain," he says. Oh, yes—our beautiful white-stone villa on top of the Aley Mountain overlooking the city of Beirut, surrounded by acres of cedar trees. I love the villa—the place where we gathered with grandparents and aunts and uncles and cousins and picked grapes and apples and watched the grown-ups get drunk and act funny.

"When will you be leaving?" my mom asks.

"Next week," he replies. "They will pay me in a month."

There is a silence, and then he adds, "I went to collect some of our money from our friends today, but no one believes we are broke. Everybody thinks that our drawers are full of cash."

After my dad leaves home, our life changes for good. It takes him months to come visit us; his visits are short, and life is stressful and dull without him. The summer comes and goes, and we do not go to the mountain that year.

How could he leave me? My stomach is tightening again.

Thank you for reliving my Marker story with me. Our bankruptcy and the death of my father were the greatest Markers in my life. They both relate to the loss of my father—first temporarily, then permanently. They were moments when something radically shifted. Daddy's little girl couldn't be Daddy's little girl anymore. The only breadwinner in our family was no longer there to take care of me. As we go through this chapter, I will return to this example to illustrate the other components we'll be unearthing. But first, it's your turn. The following exercise will guide you back into your own childhood to identify your Marker—the painful event that changed how you lived your life and who you became in the world.

This process may require some detective work, as it is not always easy to retrieve our deeply buried experiences and stories. Hold the intention to love yourself as you uncover your hidden aspects, and commit to holding the clear-eyed view throughout your plunge. Promise yourself that you will not judge, hide, avoid, or sabotage but instead, allow what is to surface and welcome it with acceptance. Through this loving approach, you can make space for your deepest experiences to surface, even the most painful ones, and simply allow them to be and acknowledge the pain that arose in your life as a consequence of those experiences. So with that in mind, let's take the nudge of our friendly dolphin as an invitation to dive deep—to look at the most painful events in your life, write them down, and relive them.

Exercise 2: Uncover Your Marker

Please read the exercise thoroughly before you begin. Open your notebook, and on a clean page near the beginning, write the heading "My Identity Signature." You will be coming back to this page and adding each component as it is uncovered. Then turn to a fresh page for this exercise, and write out the questions below in your notebook before proceeding.

Step 1

Sit quietly and move into a state of relaxation. I recommend using the Clear Lagoon visualization we created in chapter two (p. 20). After you are established here, breathe deeper and deeper.

Step 2

Breathe deeper and deeper, and then ask yourself the questions below. Ask each question three times and wait for the answer to arise.

a. *What is the most painful, scary, earth-shattering event that occurred in my life?*
b. *What is the earliest painful event that happened in my childhood, as far as I can remember?*

You may find that many events rush into your memory. Allow them to surface and then focus on them, one by one.

Step 3

You may notice a particularly vivid and painful memory, one that you have difficulty focusing on due to the discomfort. Stay with this image; breathe in the fresh air, and breathe out the pain. Look at the situation closely, and continue asking yourself these questions:

a. *What happened? When did it happen? Why did it happen?*
b. *How did I feel about it back then?*
c. *How do I feel about it now?*

Stay with the event as long as you need to. Try to remember and write down in your notebook as many details as you can recall. Focus on the sensory experiences: What did you see, hear, taste, touch, or smell? Feel the feelings that arise instead of trying to remember them. Find a way of simply being with them and noticing them. Don't be alarmed if you cry. Let it be, don't judge it, acknowledge it, and name the emotions. Be sure to write these down. We will come back to them later in this chapter.

Should you remember more than one event, as I did, it's important to write down each of them. Focus particularly on the most painful one and on the earliest one. They may be the same, but if not, write them both. You may have more than two.

STEP 4

Once you've written the long, detailed version, list your Marker(s) chronologically:

My Marker event #1 is: My father's bankruptcy
My Marker event #2 is: The death of my father

You may write down as many Marker events as you want. There are no right or wrong ways to answer this question. The beauty of this work is that you are just doing it for yourself. No one is watching you. No one is judging you. Just be sure not to judge yourself, and stay in the flow. Wherever you land is the right place for you to be right now. Once your process is launched, it will take you deeper, and you will uncover more layers of your past. So don't worry if you feel you did not find your Marker, or if you found more than one. If you have several marker events, they may be related through a similar theme, which you can use to sum them up. For example, I refer to my Marker as "the loss of my father," which relates to both events.

STEP 5

When you feel confident that you have identified your Marker, turn back to your Identity Signature page and write in this first element:

> My name is: Micheline
> **My Emotional Logo:**
>   My Marker is: The loss of my father

Once you are done with this exercise, I suggest you take a break and do not continue with the next section until tomorrow. Details about the most significant painful event of your life may still surface. If so, let them be. You may find that you cried during the exercise or notice that you are more emotional afterward. This is all very normal; give yourself space and permission to show up as you do.

IDENTIFY YOUR STICKER: OPEN UP YOUR TRAUMATIC EMOTIONS

Your painful story has become a vibrational anchor to attract negative emotions. The more intense the emotions associated with your Marker, the more imprinted your subconscious becomes with your trauma, and the more reinforced are your opinions about yourself that arise out of these events. Therefore, it is important to identify the emotions and feelings underlying the Marker, because you can't transform a negative emotion if you can't get in touch with it. I call the traumatic emotions and feelings underlying the

Marker event "Stickers" because they stick to you and recur again and again throughout your life. Every time a threat of an event occurs in your life that is similar in nature to the Marker—whether real or imagined, large or small—these same emotions will surge to the surface.

For example, when I lost my father, both initially after his bankruptcy and then through his passing, I felt a deep emotion of sadness and an unbearable separation anxiety generated by his loss. Later in life, every time I lost something, big or small, that feeling of anxiety kicked in and I became sad. My Marker event created a recurrent emotional response.

Michael Brown, in his book *The Presence Process*, suggests that *emotion* is shorthand for *energy in motion*. He writes:

> Beneath each suppressed memory, limiting belief system, and unproductive behavior pattern is a negative emotional charge ... that is responsible for the physical, mental, and emotional states of imbalance that have reoccurred in our life experience since we departed childhood. It is also this negative emotional charge that is responsible for all our dramas and our self-medication behaviors in which we consciously and unconsciously sedate and control our life experience.[6]

When we recognize and name an emotion, it changes its appearance from energy in motion to something more specific. By naming it, we make it accessible to our perception and we can retrieve it more easily. Naming or labeling the underlying emotions we are feeling allows us to be conscious of the source of our reactions or actions.

Your emotions are your indicators of the vibrations and patterns of thoughts and beliefs within you. When your beliefs and thoughts are working well for you, you are likely to feel good about yourself and be in a balanced emotional state. On the other hand, when your beliefs and thoughts are creating negative outcomes in your life, you are likely to feel a negative emotion. This emotion is your indicator and your entryway to conscious awareness.

When there is a friction and unease, your emotions are telling you that you need to pay attention. This is why our places of greatest pain are our starting points to literally change and transform our lives. Negative emotions—like tension, discord, fear, anger, or shame—become the access points to the subconscious. The worst you feel, the more intense the signal is to guide you toward your ailment. You are being called to become consciously aware of what is happening inside you, which will lead you to transform it and heal it. In a moment, I'll be guiding you through an exercise to identify your Sticker and the part of your physical body that holds it, which I call your Vessel.

IDENTIFY YOUR VESSEL

Strong emotions are usually contained in a particular area of the body, which is where we feel the sensations that accompany them. Sensations are the physiological component of an emotional experience. Physiological reactions can help us to recognize our emotional experience. For example, you may have feelings of pain, discomfort, tension, and so on that arise when the body is reacting to being emotionally triggered. You might feel tightness along with a tingling sensation and a contraction at the same time. These sensations are important to detect and name.

When I experience my Sticker, fear, I feel this emotion in my stomach. This is my Vessel. I experience a sensation of tightness in my solar plexus. For the longest time, I suffered from fragility in my stomach: indigestion and nausea, followed by gastritis, a duodenal ulcer, and acid reflux. This all continued until I became aware that this part of my body was the hostess of anxiety and I learned to love and cherish it.

Your Vessel could be a particular organ or a symptom within a body part. It could be felt as tightness in a certain area of your body or pain, palpitation, nausea, or dizziness. This physical manifestation can become a symptom. Like the emotion, it offers us an important access point to what is happening within. At times, you may not be aware of the emotion working you up under the surface, but you cannot ignore tightness in your throat or stomach. If you pay attention to your Vessel, it will guide you to acknowledge your emotion. I ignored my stomach for a long time until I became aware that I needed to attend to the emotion triggering my physical symptoms.

Are you ready to open up to your emotional makeup? Your Marker, your Sticker, and your Vessel make up your Emotional Logo. We've already identified the Marker; now let's dive in and add the other pieces to complete the picture.

EXERCISE 3: RETRIEVE YOUR STICKER, IDENTIFY YOUR VESSEL, AND BUILD YOUR EMOTIONAL LOGO

Please read the exercise thoroughly and write out the questions in your notebook before proceeding.

STEP 1

Sit quietly and move into a state of relaxation. I recommend using the Clear Lagoon visualization we created in chapter two (p. 20). After you are established here, breathe deeper and deeper.

STEP 2

Take yourself back to your Marker event. You are now present to the most painful event of your early life. Stay with it, breathe deeper and deeper, and let the image become clear. Breathe in the fresh air and breathe out the pain. Look at the situation closely; feel it at the deepest level. Let it be. Breathe deeper and deeper.

Your Marker was the birth of your Emotional Logo. When you recall the Marker event during your deep relaxation, the emotion associated with it will be allowed to surface, and it will lead you into your subconscious.

STEP 3

I would like you to introduce a new visual here that you will be using in subsequent exercises. This visual is called "the child image," and it represents your inner child. It is simply an image of you as a child, as young as you can remember yourself. I would like you to include your child image whenever you are sitting under a tree by your Clear Lagoon preparing to do one of the exercises. You will recall this image every time you go back to your Marker and you start feeling pain. In your visualization, use your own vocabulary to tell your inner child that you love him or her and that everything will be okay. You may picture the child sitting on your lap, held in your arms, or sitting opposite you with your hand on his or her heart. Listen to the child, allow the child to tell you what he or she needs from you, and offer reassurance.

STEP 4

Your Marker, the painful childhood event you're evoking, comes accompanied by an emotion, a feeling, and a sensation. Your feelings about the event, since they are perceived thoughts, could change with time, but your Sticker emotion sticks to you. It triggers a sensation in your body, your Vessel.

Ask yourself the following questions. Ask each question three times, and wait for the answers.

a. *How did I feel back then? What was the feeling associated with the event?* It could be anger, frustration, worry, apprehension, shame, grief, sorrow, melancholy, and so on. In my case, it was fear.

b. *What is my feeling about the event right now? When I think about my Marker and the way it makes me feel, do I become aware of any particular part of my body? Is it associated with any physical sensation?* It could be tightness in a certain area of your body—pain, palpitation, nausea, or dizziness. In my case, it was tightness in my stomach. Do you remember being aware of this sensation at the time of the event, and do you still feel it when you recall the Marker? Write down the body part where you feel the sensation: this is your Vessel.

Use the sensation as a guide to take you to the deeper emotion associated with your Marker. Breathe into that sensation and relive the emotional experience. Try to describe it with the first word that comes before thinking. You may use the same language you used to describe your feelings, but you may find that the underlying emotion is different. For example, you might feel angry about something, but the underlying emotion is fear. Remember, emotions live in the body. Although they sometimes have the same names as feelings, they tend to be more primal and visceral in their nature. In my case, underlying the feelings of sadness and fear of loss was a raw emotion of fear that I felt in my tightening stomach. When you identify the emotion, write it down. This is your Sticker.

STEP 5

Turn back to your Identity Signature page and add these components to your Emotional Logo in the following format:

My name is: Micheline
My Emotional Logo:
    My Marker is: The loss of my father
    My Sticker is: Fear
    My Vessel is: My stomach

Congratulations. You have completed the most challenging, yet essential part of the process and identified your Emotional Logo. During the next few days, I recommend that you reread this chapter and repeat the exercises. Be sure to write in your journal about your emotions and thoughts. A lot of inhibited, suppressed memories may resurface along with emotions that have been repressed for a long time. Let them be, and know that this is totally normal. In fact, it is a significant step toward self-actualization and awareness. Your Emotional Logo is a key that will open the door to deeper transformative work as we move forward in this process.

EMOTIONAL AWARENESS

Distinguishing your Emotional Logo—the Marker event, the Sticker emotion, and the Vessel that hosts it in your body—allows you to feel the emotion, name it, question it, and become consciously aware of your actions in a rational way. What then becomes possible is to transform your unconscious actions and reactions into conscious responses. In so doing, you break the victim cycle and master your circumstances in life. It also allows you to transform your relationship with your own trauma and the traumatic emotion itself. Simply put, you become emotionally aware.

Without emotional awareness, the typical cycle is as follows:

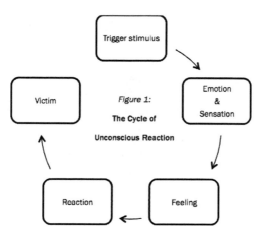

Figure 1:
The Cycle of
Unconscious Reaction

With emotional awareness, the cycle is transformed.

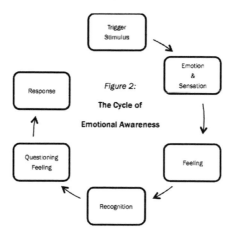

Figure 2:
The Cycle of
Emotional Awareness

5 Stage 2: Awaken to Your Beliefs

Wherever you are, you are 'here.' You are where you perceive yourself to be. Your thoughts, feelings, and beliefs create the landscape in your psyche. This is the place you truly inhabit, which can be unrelated to the place you physically inhabit.
—Collette Baron-Reid, *The Map*

Our traumatic emotions, which we've uncovered in the previous chapter, are what give rise to our Core Beliefs. Our Core Beliefs delineate who we think we are; they form our sense of identity at an unconscious level. They determine the way we live our lives and shape our actions and reactions. In this stage of the process, we will be shedding light on these beliefs in order to make them more conscious and identifying what I call your Belief Matrix, which is the next component of your Identity Signature. This includes three elements:

> **Your Verdict:** A negative opinion you sentenced yourself to following the painful Marker event in your childhood. It constitutes a judgment of yourself that you carry inside like a verdict without being aware of it.

Your Strategy: The game plan you came up with to mask your verdict.

Your Proof of Identity: The first time you successfully used your Strategy—the event that helped reinforce it and made you (and others) believe it, replacing your Verdict (your believed deficiency) with a new identity, like a mask.

As human beings, we are constantly forming thoughts that we organize into beliefs. For example: *This is good for me,* or *This is bad for me; I should do this,* or *I should shy away from that; She is better than me,* or *She is stupid; I am incompetent,* or *I am great.* And on it goes. These comparisons and judgments coalesce into beliefs. In this work, I am particularly interested in those very stubborn limiting beliefs that play in the background, outside of our awareness, and limit our openness, our growth, and our development. These obstinate, negative beliefs find their roots in childhood and become subconscious and therefore very hard to access.

When we are young, our minds are vulnerable and easily influenced by our parents, or those who raised us, and what they tell us verbally or non-verbally. We emulate some of their behaviors and act like them at times without having developed the capacity to understand our behaviors. We are like sponges receiving raw data as true, without any capacity to edit or select it; therefore, it imprints us deeply. We believe the information even more than our parents, who might have chosen to believe in some of it. We mirror their positive or negative thoughts and emulate their positive or negative behaviors without discernment.

For the purposes of our work, I would like to distinguish two types of Core Beliefs:

1. The Core Beliefs we have formed about ourselves. These are created either because of a conviction we had about

ourselves or because we bought into someone else's belief about us and internalized it.

2. The Core Beliefs we formed about everybody and everything else. These beliefs were acquired from our environment, from our parents or the people who raise us, from schoolteachers, from childhood friends, from our religious communities, from our family or neighborhood friends, from the media.

In this work, we will be focusing on our beliefs about ourselves, but once you have learned this process, you will also be able to apply it to the beliefs you have about others.

Our beliefs are formed by what we learn; they are shaped by our experiences early on and by what we interpreted our experiences to mean. Our personal, unique experiences make our belief systems unique. Since beliefs are so primordial to how we live our lives, I do encourage you to question them every step of the way, especially those that are negative in nature. None of us aim to live a mediocre life, but many of us resign ourselves to mediocrity, even though we are capable of living a great life, because we are stuck in our inner beliefs about ourselves.

Your belief system becomes your main filter for perception as you store information and form more beliefs. Any information that comes through is filtered according to the following criteria:

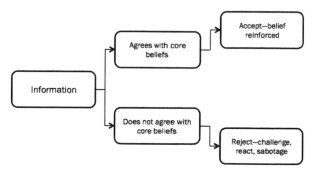

Figure 3: How Beliefs Filter Information

Some of us are so deeply impacted by our negative Core Belief system about ourselves that we can even sabotage a positive event that happens to us because it does not agree with our Core Belief.

The following story exemplifies the power of Core Beliefs. Sam was a dear neighbor of ours who fundamentally believed he was poor. His whole life had been about money struggles and the belief that he never had enough. His pattern was to build wealth and then lose it overnight. His last project was building a furniture-manufacturing company that became global. Despite his success, Sam still did not believe that he was wealthy. I remember having lengthy discussions with him, trying to convince him that he could afford to pay for his kid's college or even a vacation—to no avail. One day, his factory caught on fire, and he lost his inventory. Because he was a hard worker and he believed that he had nothing, it was easy for him to rebuild it from scratch. Between the insurance money and his dedicated employees, he rebuilt his empire again. But when the money was too good to be true for his belief, Sam managed to lose everything again. He got into a bad deal with his partner, signing off the business to him and collateralizing it against bonds that tanked soon after. It was a simple error of judgment, but it agreed all too well with Sam's Core Belief: "I am poor."

Not only do we disbelieve that which does not sit well with our inner beliefs; we may even unknowingly sabotage our way out of happiness or success if it does not agree with us. We keep repeating mistake after mistake and may never become aware of it, even after a serious crisis. We simply become bitter and more entrenched in our beliefs. I recently heard spiritual teacher Carolyn Myss on a radio show speaking to this very point. In her assertive voice, she said: "Crisis serves us to become bitter or better ..."

To you, the reader, I ask: bitter or better? Which way do you want to go?

If your answer is "better," let's go back to your earliest crisis, your Marker, and expose the core negative belief you created out of it: your Verdict.

EXPOSE YOUR VERDICT

The Verdict is the negative opinion you sentenced yourself to, following that painful event in your childhood you've identified as your Marker. It constitutes a judgment of yourself that you carry inside without being aware of it. It is your most disliked thought, coupled with an emotion you have about yourself. It is the darkest belief that you harbor in a hidden place inside. It constitutes your basic lie, like an original sin. Identifying a Core Belief is like solving a mystery in your mind. You have to dive deep below the recurring limiting thoughts to find the hidden beliefs.

The Verdict is the reason why you decided to show up in the world a certain way. Behind every pattern of behavior, there is a Core Belief about oneself or about the world. Some are really helpful, giving rise to smart strategies based on rational thinking. The Verdict I would like to tackle here, however, is the one that finds its origin in fear, not in love. It is the verdict that came as a result of a big emotional shock, found a permanent dwelling-place in your mind, and decided to run its operations from your subconscious. It hacked your inner self and started directing your actions, while you denied its existence and buried it under many layers. Your core limiting patterns were created as a result of this belief.

The Verdict is usually associated with an internal negative judgment that you made about yourself. Perhaps you deemed yourself unacceptable, inferior, or even evil. Perhaps you concluded you were a victim of people or circumstances, subject to injustice. Even when you feel good about yourself, this little voice haunts you and tells you not to believe the good stuff because it has evidence to the contrary.

In my case, my Verdict stemmed from the belief that I couldn't make it on my own. Abandoned by my father, I judged myself weak and inferior. My Verdict became "I am not capable enough." I was ashamed of this feeling. I wanted to bury it deep down and hide it from everybody, especially from myself.

Your Verdict about yourself limits your higher potential. At a fundamental level, it colors your perceptions, creates your projections onto others, and sets up filters between you and reality. It is buried deep and ingrained in you. It may be hidden from your view, like a car in your blind spot, but it may surface from time to time. When it does, it makes you so uncomfortable that you deny it, bury it deeper, or bypass it. It is like a buoy that you would like to keep underwater but keeps pushing itself upward. The more you try to push it down, the more it resists, until you lose your grip. As the author Debbie Ford said, "What we cannot be with does not let us be."[7]

The Verdict is your darkest and most unwanted aspect of your self. Despite entombing it deep in your subconscious, it remains the most powerful engine driving your life, the source of your operating system. Are you ready to bring it into the light of consciousness? Let's dive in.

Exercise 4: Expose Your Verdict

Please read the exercise thoroughly and write the questions in your notebook before proceeding.

Open your notebook to your Identity Signature page and review your Emotional Logo before you start your breathing and visualization exercise.

Step 1

Sit quietly and move into a state of relaxation. I recommend using the Clear Lagoon visualization we created in chapter two (p. 20). Once you are established there, breathe deeper and deeper.

Step 2

Take yourself back to your Marker event. You are now present to the most painful event of your early life. Stay with it,

breathe deeper and deeper, and imagine yourself as the little child you were back then. Stay with the image; let it become clear. Breathe in the fresh air and breathe out the pain. Look at the situation closely; feel it at the deepest level. Let it be. Breathe deeper and deeper.

STEP 3

Call upon your child image as you are sitting under the tree by your Clear Lagoon.

STEP 4

Call upon the Sticker emotion that is associated with your Marker event. Feel the emotion and the sensation in your body; visualize yourself back there with vivid detail. How old were you? What happened? Why did it happen? Stay with the emotion, let it be, and start breathing again deeper and deeper.

STEP 5

Ask yourself the following questions. Ask each question three times and wait for the answer.

a. *How do I feel about my Marker now? Do I still feel the sensation in my body when I remember the event? Do I still feel it in the same place? How strong is the sensation?*

b. *What did I tell myself about myself back then?*

c. *What is it about me that no one knows, but I fear that if they knew, they would run away from me?*

d. *What is it about me that is so horrible I am hiding it from everyone?*

Is there a common theme to your answers? If so, see if you can phrase this in a sentence beginning "I am ..." Often, the Verdict takes the form of a "not enough" statement, e.g., "I am not strong enough," or "I am not lovable enough." Write down a sentence like this that describes the thing you are hiding about yourself.

STEP 6

Turn to your Identity Signature page and begin a new section beneath your Emotional Logo entitled My Belief Matrix. Record your Verdict here, like this:

My name is: Micheline
My Emotional Logo:
　　My Marker is: The loss of my father
　　My Sticker is: Fear
　　My Vessel is: My stomach
My Belief Matrix:
　　My Verdict is: I am not capable enough.

UNDERSTAND YOUR STRATEGY

When we come to a negative Verdict about ourselves early in life—something we are so ashamed of that we want to hide it from the world—it is natural that we quickly come up with a Strategy to ensure that no one will ever know what's buried inside. The Strategy is a game plan to cover up the Verdict. It's the mask we create and display to the world. Once we enact our Strategy, we move our process from an internal one to an external one. Our beliefs are now being expressed in the world and are affecting ourselves and others.

For example, in my case, I needed to show the world that I was the opposite of weak and incapable. I remember the day I had to go back to school, after my dad went bankrupt. My mom told me she could not afford to buy me books. I decided to take charge, to take matters in my own hands. I gathered my books and my siblings' books from the previous year and headed to the market. I sold them all and bought used copies of all the books on the school list. I came back with them all, except one that I could not find, and I had a bit of extra cash in my pocket as well. My mom was really happy and relieved, and I was, too. My Strategy—"be super responsible"—seemed to have worked. Unfortunately, my newfound confidence took a hit the next day when the snobbish nun reminded me that I did not order my books through the school and my classmate insisted on comparing her new, clean version of the science book to my old, underlined one. I was ashamed and did not feel good enough, despite the fact that my grades turned out to be far better than hers. However, I persisted with my Strategy. And when my second Marker event occurred, with my father's death, I concluded that to survive this loss, I had only one way to go. It was the promise I whispered to my dead father.

I will be strong, be responsible for my family, provide for them financially, deny my own grief. One strategy: be super-responsible.

This promise found its expression in so many aspects of my life. I wanted to prove myself in everything I did—to prove myself to others, but mainly to myself. But I definitely ran out of fuel at one point because my Verdict—the judgmental little voice in my head—would make sure that whatever I did was "not enough."

It acted up at work, at home, in my relationships. I always did more than I was expected to do. It even acted up in the little things like working around the house or inviting people over. When my friends and family would come for dinner, they were always surprised at the amount of food I would prepare for them. Despite this abundance, I would be convinced that there was not enough food for everybody. I kept running like crazy to prove this little voice wrong.

The quality and intensity of the Sticker emotion associated with your Marker predetermines the intensity of your Verdict and the power of your coping Strategy. When you first felt the emotion of pain, you assessed it cognitively and sensed it physiologically, which started a biological chain of reactions, such as an increased heart rate or pituitary adrenal response. You decided how to react to reduce the pain. The first reaction is: *never again*. For example, "I never again want to feel this pain associated with my vulnerability," or "never again will I live through the pain of being not enough." Therefore, there is a powerful drive behind the need to take charge and become the person who is needed by everyone else, thus ensuring I will never experience being alone.

The development of your Strategy is not a rational act—it is a survival impulse. It is like running away from danger under severe fear and pressure. You feel the emotion of fear, your heart pounds, and you scream and run. Your reaction is a coping strategy. When similar threats happen to you, you will not stop and think about how to respond; you will simply repeat your strategy and reinforce it.

Your Strategy becomes a mask and a motivator to hide your Verdict and keep it imprisoned inside. Of course, it doesn't always succeed. A point is often reached that is sometimes called the "dark night of the soul"—a deep crisis. Perhaps you lose your job, go through a divorce, lose your house, or get diagnosed with a major illness. All of a sudden, you are thrown to your knees, and this bewitching voice in your head takes over. This is when your Strategy faces its biggest test and fails. Life, at some point, will give you the opportunity to see beyond your Strategy and become aware of your Verdict, but you may not listen to it. Instead, you may become more convinced of your victimhood and use your crisis to get pity and blame others and the universe for it. It is up to you. We will discuss moments like this and how to navigate them in chapter eight. For now, let's dive in and shed light on your Strategy.

Exercise 5: Understand Your Strategy

Please read the exercise thoroughly and write the questions in your notebook before proceeding.

Open your notebook to your Identity Signature page and review your Emotional Logo before you start your breathing and visualization exercise.

Step 1

Sit quietly and move into a state of relaxation. I recommend using the Clear Lagoon visualization we created in chapter two (p. 20). Once you are established there, breathe deeper and deeper.

Step 2

Take yourself back to your Marker event. You are now present to the most painful event of your early life. Breathe deeper and deeper, and imagine yourself as the little child you were back then. Stay with the image; let it become clear. Breathe in the fresh air and breathe out the pain. Look at the situation closely; feel it at the deepest level. Let it be. Breathe deeper and deeper.

Step 3

Call upon your child image as you are sitting under the tree by your Clear Lagoon.

Step 4

Call upon the Sticker emotion that is associated with your Marker event. Feel the emotion and the sensation in your body; visualize yourself back there with vivid detail. How old were you? What happened? Why did it happen? Stay with the emotion, let it be, and start breathing again, deeper and deeper.

STEP 5

What was the decision that you made at this time in your life, in order to survive? In order to *never experience this again*? What did you decide to become? Your Strategy is usually a statement beginning with a verb, such as *be* or *become*. Write it down.

STEP 6

Turn to your Identity Signature page and record your Strategy, like this:

> My name is: Micheline
> My Emotional Logo:
>> My Marker is: The loss of my father
>> My Sticker is: Fear
>> My Vessel is: My stomach
> My Belief Matrix:
>> My Verdict is: I am not capable enough.
>> My Strategy is: Be super-responsible

UNEARTH YOUR PROOF OF IDENTITY

Your Strategy gets reinforced through repetition. When you enact it over and over again, successfully, your Strategy becomes a pattern that you identify with. You begin to believe that *it is you*. It masks the Verdict and becomes your identity. Early in this process, there is usually a key moment when the success of your Strategy is confirmed. It may be the first time you repeat it and it works, at a key juncture in your life. It may be a particularly pivotal life event when your Strategy convinces everyone around you. It becomes fixed. I call this moment your Proof of Identity. It is a moment that served to reinforce your Strategy and made you believe it. It replaced your Verdict and started to disguise your believed deficiency. Through repetition, it became reinforced and came to seem so plausible that you may have even forgotten its origins.

Your Proof of Identity was the birth of who you we are choosing to become in the world, and it turned into the core pattern that is the theme of your life, as we will see in the next chapter. Here is the story of my Proof of Identity—the moment I convinced myself and those around me that I was "super-responsible."

My Proof of Identity

It is thundering outside, but it is more than thunder. Terrifying shrieks and explosions are all around us. The Syrian army and the Palestinian militia are shelling the Christian areas of Beirut and concentrating their effort on the Hotel-Dieu hospital, which happens to be on the same trajectory as our building. We hear crying in the dark. My family and I are all hiding in my small room below the staircase. I feel like fainting, but I have to be strong for my mom and my siblings. It's a test of character that is so out of character for me—to be submissive. But at this moment, all that we can do is hide and pray that the bombs will miss our building. Eventually, I take my pillow and go lay in the bathtub. It feels kind of safe to me, protected by walls. I surrender to sleep.

It's been like this every night for the past few days. I fall asleep to the sound of shelling, and I wake up to the sirens of fire trucks and ambulances. I am nineteen years old, a nursing student at the American University of Beirut. I have a scholarship and a stipend, which supports my family. Our campus is located in East Beirut, but I came home to West Beirut before the bombardment began, and now I'm not sure I can make it back across the border alive. Abandoning my studies temporarily, I have been volunteering in the local community center, putting my rudimentary nursing skills into practice. And I have fallen in love. My first love—a tall, dark-haired young man with beautiful eyes who talks to me about the stars, writes love notes to me on the chalkboard, and kisses me as we huddle in a doorway hiding from gunfire.

Today, when I arrive at the community center, excited to see my boyfriend and feeling important and needed in the midst of the crisis, the phone rings. It is the dean of the nursing school.

"Micheline, my dear," she says, "we understand the tragic circumstances of West Beirut but if you do not report back to school tomorrow, we will drop you out of the semester."

My protests fall on deaf ears. No matter that crossing the border between West and East Beirut could end my life with a sniper's bullet. Not going will cost me my place in school—and my stipend, which my family relies on. A familiar crippling feeling takes over my stomach. All my options are losers at this point. How can I leave my family and risk not seeing them again soon, not being able to help them if they get hurt, or even being hurt or be killed trying to cross to West Beirut under the snipers' bullets? But if I don't leave them, I can't help them out financially. And how can I leave my boyfriend, whom I am starting to love? But how can I risk my career if I don't leave?

The threat of all these losses is triggering the fear that stems from the Marker event of my dad's loss. A sudden anxiety attack with sharp stomach pains grips me. I feel sick to my stomach. I run to the restroom and throw up, while a rush of negative thoughts overtakes me. I'm clearly "not capable enough" to handle the situation. I wish my dad were here. Should I pray to Jesus again? But he didn't help him. I'm on my own. I've got to make a decision.

I certainly can't show my weakness to the world. I'm a nurse, treating the injured. My family relies on me. Ignoring the clenching in my stomach, I summon up the commitment I made to my dad. I need to graduate to help my family. This is who I am: I'm super-responsible.

In no time, I have informed my boyfriend of my intention to go back to school by the next morning. The rest of the plan is relatively easy to achieve compared to bearing his disappointment and sadness. The next day, braving random bullets, unfriendly checkpoints, and the occasional mortar blast, I miraculously make it safely to West Beirut. I am back in school. My stipend is safe. My family will have food on the table. My Strategy worked. It has been proven. This is my identity; this is who I am.

Thank you for listening to my story. I hope it serves to illustrate how a Verdict gives rise to a Strategy, which becomes reinforced by a Proof of Identity, masking the original Verdict and hiding it from oneself and the world. The fact that I stepped into my father's shoes at age nineteen and provided for my family, even if it meant risking my own life, cemented the Strategy I'd been employing since my father's death. It proved to me that this was my new identity, and it also proved it to the people around me. My brave and risky choice convinced everyone that I was the very opposite of my Verdict. Are you ready to find out what that moment was for you—to unearth your Proof of Identity? Let's dive in.

EXERCISE 6: UNEARTH YOUR PROOF OF IDENTITY

Please read the exercise thoroughly and write the questions in your notebook before proceeding.

Open your notebook to your Identity Signature page and review your Emotional Logo before you start your breathing and visualization exercise.

STEP 1

Sit quietly and move into a state of relaxation. I recommend using the Clear Lagoon visualization we created in chapter two (p. 20). Once you are established there, breathe deeper and deeper.

STEP 2

Take yourself back to your Marker event. You are now present to the most painful event of your early life. Stay with it,

breathe deeper and deeper, and imagine yourself as the little child you were back then. Stay with the image; let it become clear. Breathe in the fresh air, and breathe out the pain. Look at the situation closely; feel it at the deepest level. Let it be. Breathe deeper and deeper.

Step 3

Call upon your child image as you are sitting under the tree by your Clear Lagoon.

Step 4

Call upon the Sticker emotion that is associated with your Marker event. Feel the emotion and the sensation in your body; visualize yourself back there in vivid detail. How old were you? What happened? Why did it happen? Stay with the emotion, let it be, and start breathing again, deeper and deeper.

Step 5

Think about your Strategy. Among the many times in your life when you enacted your Strategy, what was the first time you clearly remember your Strategy being noticed by your family, friends, colleagues, or community? It does not have to be a heroic act; it could be something small but noticeable, like the first time you were needed, or put yourself in charge, or made a critical decision. When did you and others start to believe your Strategy? If you can, sum up your Proof of Identity in a single sentence. For example, for me, "stepping into my father's shoes at age nineteen" against all odds, even in the face of snipers, was my proof that I was super-responsible. Write it down.

STEP 6

Turn to your Identity Signature page and record your Proof of Identity, like this:

My name is: Micheline
My Emotional Logo:
> My Marker is: The loss of my father
> My Sticker is: Fear
> My Vessel is: My stomach

My Belief Matrix:
> My Verdict is: I am not capable enough
> My Strategy is: Be super-responsible
> My Proof of Identity is: Stepping into my father's shoes at age nineteen

You have now completed your Belief Matrix. Through these exercises, you have shed light on the beliefs that became solidified into an identity and gave rise to your core patterns of behavior, as we will explore in the chapter that follows.

6 Stage 3: Name Your Patterns

Now is the time to examine our past a bit more, to take a look at some of the beliefs that have been running us. Some people find this part of the cleansing process very painful, but it need not be. We must look at what is there before we can clean it out.
—Louise L. Hay, *You Can Heal Your Life*

Let's recap where we've come so far in our process. You've uncovered the traumatic Marker event that gave rise to powerful emotions that stayed with you as Stickers, which are carried in your physical body in a particular Vessel. These are the elements of your Emotional Logo. These events gave rise to a system of beliefs. The traumatic effect of your Marker event made you draw a particular conclusion about yourself, a Verdict. Believing your Verdict led you to come up with a Strategy, which was reinforced by a Proof of Identity. These are the elements of your Belief Matrix.

Now, we will take the next step and look at how all of this has created what I call your Behavior Patterns. There are two elements to this final component:

> **Your Core Pattern:** Your Core Pattern is your life theme. It is a bold, persistent, and recurrent theme of behavior you have enacted throughout your life,

which arose out of your Belief Matrix. It directs your attitudes and impacts the important decisions that you make. It pre-determines your reactions and your decisions.

Your Shadow Pattern: A repressed, denied, mostly invisible pattern of behavior that represents the shadow side of you.

IDENTIFY YOUR CORE PATTERN

Human beings are pattern-forming creatures. In order to make sense of the world, we look for repeating occurrences in phenomena around us. We try to discern the rationale behind repeating events and processes. The same happens with our inner worlds. We have patterns of thoughts and beliefs, which dictate our patterns of behavior. Despite these many different yet interlocked patterns, it seems that most of us have a predominant one—the pattern that arises from our Emotional Logo and our Identity Signature. I am calling this the Core Pattern because it drives our most important actions. In this chapter, we will be identifying your Core Pattern and examining how it was formed. When you understand the structure of your Core Pattern, it enables you to cultivate awareness of your actions and to transform your reactions into responses.

Your Strategy was a decision you made to show the world the opposite of your Verdict—the negative judgment that you secretly believe. You cemented your Strategy for yourself and the world through your Proof of Identity. When you express and repeat your Strategy over and over again and become proficient at it, it becomes a Core Pattern. Your Strategy is no longer a decision; it is a habit. What started as a declaration to get yourself out of a harsh reality has now blended itself with who you think you are and who the world around you thinks you are. Therefore, the world around you becomes your mirror; it reflects back at you the image you project into it and confirms its reality.

In my case, for example, I am now convinced that I am a super-responsible being, and the world around me is convinced of that as well. It is no longer something I have to remind myself to do ("be super-responsible")—it has fully become my Core Pattern, so I gave it a name: "Superwoman." I like to use names as opposed to actions to label the Core Pattern, because doing so highlights the difference between a deliberate strategy and a habitual pattern. Your Strategy should be able to complete a sentence beginning "I will … " such as: "I will be super-responsible." But your Core Pattern should be able to complete a sentence beginning "I am …"

Your Strategy started out as a great plan that allowed you to get by when times were tough. It came in handy and gave you the illusion that you were protecting yourself. In turn, your Core Pattern allowed your heroic actions; your creativity; your soul, mind, and spirit; and your experiences to express themselves within a frame. It is like an energetic structure of fulfillment for your expression in the world. It has been a winning strategy that has helped you be successful, but it has also, at some point, created certain limitations to who you can be. It has determined your inner conditioning and limited your expression in the world. It has become your internal software and created an ingrained pattern of safety and security, which keeps you from taking risks or venturing into uncharted waters. Your Core Pattern may seem positive, but it found its roots in the negative Verdict that you decided to hide from yourself and the world. Therefore, as in my case, it originated from fear and survival instincts. It has had survival advantages: it helped repair a negative self-image and projected an opposite image into the world.

In reality, the major flaw of your Core Pattern is that it is a control freak, and you are not even aware of it. It controls your life and occupies the driver's seat while giving you the illusion that you are the driver. Its origin is now completely hidden, like a car in the blind spot of your mirror.

It may work for a while, but sooner or later, you will find

yourself repeating the same neurosis you are trying to cover up and getting into the same situations. Uncovering your Core Pattern, knowing it and labeling it, will enable you to have control over it instead of it controlling you. It will help you shift your Strategy from being on autopilot to manual—giving it a switch that you can power off, so long as you recognize it in time. While you will not be able to get rid of your Core Pattern, you will be able to acknowledge it, characterize it, and disempower it through conscious awareness. Understanding your Core Pattern allows you to become more intimate with yourself. Self-intimacy is what precedes self-love; it also precedes understanding others and your capacity to love others. It is the major ingredient of self-awareness and the precursor to conscious evolution. Are you ready to get more intimate with yourself? Let's dive in.

Exercise 7: Identify Your Core Pattern

Please read the exercise thoroughly and write out the questions in your notebook before proceeding.

Open your notebook to your Identity Signature page and review it before you start your breathing and visualization exercise.

Step 1

Sit quietly and move into a state of relaxation. I recommend using the Clear Lagoon visualization we created in chapter two (p. 20). Once you are established there, breathe deeper and deeper.

Step 2

Take yourself back to your Marker event. You are now present to the most painful event of your early life. Stay with it,

breathe deeper and deeper, and imagine yourself as the little child you were back then. Stay with the image; let it become clear. Breathe in the fresh air and breathe out the pain. Look at the situation closely; feel it at the deepest level. Let it be. Breathe deeper and deeper.

STEP 3

Call upon your child image as you are sitting under the tree by your Clear Lagoon.

STEP 4

Call upon the Sticker emotion that is associated with your Marker event. Feel the emotion and the sensation in your body; visualize yourself back there in vivid detail. How old were you? What happened? Why did it happen? Stay with the emotion, let it be, and keep breathing, deeper and deeper.

STEP 5

Ask yourself the following questions. Ask each question three times and wait for the answer:

a. *Who did I become as a direct result of my Marker? What was my Strategy of survival? Do I still operate the same way when faced with a crisis?*

List any examples you can think of where you reacted to a specific crisis.

b. *Is there a common denominator to these events? Is there a sort of modus operandi that I can derive? If so, what is it?*

c. *How would I define myself in terms of my contribution to others?*

For example: responsible friend, loving partner, dedicated associate, and accountable employee. Write down the answers and notice if there is a common theme that labels you in the world. If you had to choose one attribute that would describe you, what would that be?

d. *Am I known by people around me to display certain characteristics? What would they label me?*

Put yourself in the shoes of the other people in your life. Think about your partner, your family, your friends, and your colleagues. What name would they give you? For example, if you tend to give too much and put other people before yourself, do people think of you as "Mother Teresa"? In my case, I am the person who will deal with any problem given to me. My Strategy of being super-responsible became my Core Pattern of being "Superwoman."

See if you can find a name that captures the theme that was emerging in your answers above—a word or phrase that could describe you to complete the sentence "I am ..." Congratulations, you have uncovered your Core Pattern. Write it down.

Step 6

Turn to your Identity Signature page and begin a new section beneath your Emotional Logo and your Belief Matrix, called "My Behavior Patterns." Record your Core Pattern here, like this:

My name is: Micheline
My Emotional Logo:
    My Marker is: The loss of my father
    My Sticker is: Fear
    My Vessel is: My stomach
My Belief Matrix:
    My Verdict is: I am not capable enough
    My Strategy is: Be super-responsible
    My Proof of Identity is: Stepping into my father's
        shoes at age nineteen
My Behavior Patterns:
    My Core Pattern is: Superwoman

STEP 7.

Over the next few days, you may find it interesting to validate your Core Pattern with the people around you. Ask your partner, your siblings, your relatives, your colleagues, or your boss how you appear to them. If they were to use one word to describe you, what would it be? In most cases, how people describe you is similar or even better than the way you describe yourself. In the event that your findings are much more positive and diverge significantly from your Core Pattern, I encourage you then to re-read this part of the chapter and do the exercises again.

IS THERE A RELATIONSHIP BETWEEN OUR CORE PATTERNS AND ARCHETYPES?

You may notice that when you identify your Core Pattern, it reflects what some people would consider an "archetypal" image, such as that of the hero, the warrior, or the savior. Psychologists refer to archetypes as patterns of thought or identity that live in our collective unconscious and express themselves through individuals.

Carl Jung was one of the first to make a distinction between the personal unconscious and the collective unconscious, with the collective unconscious containing the inherited psychic structures and archetypal images that have universal meanings—the heritage of our human evolution.

Could archetypes be the reason why our Core Patterns tend to take certain forms? For example, the mythical archetypes provide us with symbols that can shed light and give us deep insights into our own patterns.

Carolyn Myss illustrated these principles in her book *The Archetypes*. Myss traces back the origin of the archetypes to the Divine and thinks that an archetype is part of a person's "spiritual chronology," which constitutes sacred contracts that were established prior to birth and organize our creativity, our strategies, and our psyche. She identifies ten primary archetypes:

- The Advocate
- The Artist/Creative
- The Athlete
- The Caregiver
- The Fashionista
- The Intellectual
- The Queen/Executive
- The Rebel
- The Spiritual Seeker
- The Visionary.

Do you recognize any of these in yourself?

RECOGNIZE YOUR SHADOW PATTERN

Your Core Pattern represents the positive image of yourself that you want to project to the world. But there is always another side to every picture—a hidden part of the self that you are trying to mask and conceal. Carl Jung named this hidden part of us the Shadow. Our shadow also contains patterns of beliefs and behaviors, and just as we have a Core Pattern that represents the image of ourselves we have created to mask the Verdict, we also have a Shadow Pattern that represents that hidden Verdict and threatens to reveal it to the world.

The Shadow Pattern is the dark side of the ego: the repressed, denied, and hidden part of each one of us. While the Core Pattern is the social mask we wear in our daily lives to project an attractive image in the world, the Shadow Pattern contains those predominant characteristics that we push away and keep buried under the surface. It represents the weakest, most undesirable, negative, hideous parts of ourselves that we remain insecure about, no matter how prosperous, attractive, lovely, spiritual, or famous we become. We avoid showing our jealousy, greed, lust, shame, hatred, violence, betrayal, addiction, and so on. The Shadow Pattern, which is hidden from awareness, contains our self-destructive behaviors. The major distinction between a Core Pattern and a Shadow Pattern is that the first is visible (although its roots are hidden), whereas the second is invisible but pops up inadvertently when triggered by an emotion.

I love this poem from the Indian poet Rabindranath Tagore, which expresses what it is like to live with one's Shadow:

> I came out alone on my way to my tryst.
> But who is this that follows me in the silent dark?
> I move aside to avoid his presence but I escape him not.
> He makes the dust rise from the earth with his swagger;
> he adds his loud voice to every word I utter.
> He is my own little self, my lord, he knows no shame;
> but I am ashamed to come to thy door in his company.[8]

Because we deny ourselves an outlet for our Shadow Patterns, we often tend to project our negative qualities onto others. If you think about the people in your life whom you strongly dislike, you may find that they represent a piece of yourself that you don't like and don't want to see.

As long as we don't acknowledge the darker side in ourselves, we can't acknowledge the darker side in others. This explains why some romantic relationships fall apart when they become more intimate. In the first phase of infatuation, we tend to overlook the Shadow side of the other person, just as we deny our own. But when we move in together, for example, and start sharing every moment, we suddenly can't avoid the aspects of the other person that we have been denying.

As long as we are avoiding the Shadow, we can't be whole and we can't contribute to creating wholeness in the world. Recognizing our dual self, our dual patterns, will help us be more intimate with ourselves and will make us capable of intimacy with others. Therefore, to become whole is to acknowledge all of it—the good, the bad, and the ugly. We must learn to greet it with no resistance and own it, as it really belongs to us.

As the collective unconscious is expressed in Core Patterns, it is also reflected in the Shadow Pattern. Families, businesses, governments, religious groups, and other organizations all have their own shadows. The hidden scandals that come to the surface every once in a while are manifestations of the shadow of these organizations.

A TALE OF TWO PATTERNS

Years ago, I encountered two individuals whose story provides a powerful illustration of the power of the Core Pattern and the Shadow Pattern, as well as all the elements we have discussed so far in this book.

It began when I attended a workshop on energy healing in Florida, led by a well-known healer named Jeffrey. He was a powerful teacher—the kind of person who seems to be able to see through you, who tells you facts about your life that no one else knew and gives you insights on how to heal from physical or psychological pain. He could tell each of us exactly what we were writing about, thinking, doing, or reading, even from a distance. He was an impressive human being who has done a lot of good work for many people. He could make people cry and laugh in a split second, and he would dive deep with them until they touched the source of their pain. He called himself a "psychic surgeon." At one point in the workshop, we all witnessed an eighty-five-year-old lady forgive her mother and feel the power of her love as he was able to tell her things no one knew about their relationship and give her signs that only she was able to decipher. We were all respectful of his heightened abilities of clairvoyance, as he certainly seemed able to access information we could not see.

Years later, Jeffrey passed away, and I kept in touch with his assistant, Leslie, a seventy-year-old lady who had helped him create and deliver his workshops. Leslie was a retired professor who spoke multiple languages and was well versed in many different religions and philosophies. When Jeffrey fell ill, Leslie had moved in with him to be by his side. I remembered how during his workshops, Jeffrey had been very assertive with Leslie, to put it nicely. He ordered her around like a puppet. She was a beautiful old woman with the nicest smile, who always said thank you a million times for the little things anyone did for her. She was frail and almost crippled. Her hands were distorted and crooked, and she had a huge hump on her back like Quasimodo in Victor Hugo's classic book, *The Hunchback of Notre Dame*. During one workshop, Jeffrey insisted that she swim in the cold ocean despite her fear of water, and we all cheered her power and tenacity.

I was surprised by how advanced Jeffrey was in the psychic realm and how primitive his level of emotional maturity seemed to be, as evidenced in his treatment of Leslie. When I confronted him about his underlying anger and the way he treated Leslie, he refuted it and said that this was part of his methodology to wake up the brain. Leslie corroborated his excuse and asked me not to intervene or help her out. He, in turn, told me that I was licking the wounds of his assistant and identifying with her instead of helping her to get out of her brain and change her mode of operation. I must admit that I believed him at the time, but my gut was not at ease with his answers.

Leslie came over to visit me after her teacher had passed. I was moved that she traveled so far by herself, given her age and physical disability. We sat down comfortably in the living room and then Leslie asked me if she could experience the Dolphin's DANCE process. I asked her if she was willing to handle what she might come across during her deep dive, and she said she was absolutely ready. I put pillows around her to support her aching body, and we began.

Because she was a regular meditator and had done years of therapy and transformational workshops, Leslie was quickly able to dive deep and go back in time and become conscious of her first trauma in life. In less than five minutes, she retrieved her Marker and was able to describe it vividly. Her mother had been physically abusive of her and would beat her hard every time she made a mistake. Leslie recalled her earliest memory of this abuse. Her mother convinced her that she was not capable of carrying out any task on her own. The emotion associated with it, her Sticker, was fear—a crippling terror that almost paralyzed her. Her Vessel was her back. Because she was ashamed of herself, she hid her face and bowed down as she was walking through life. She had become so convinced that her mother was right that she had developed a tiny voice that could barely be heard, as she was convinced that what came out of her mouth was nonsense. She was not capable of carrying any task on her own. This was clearly her Verdict through life, and she remained convinced, even though she had a PhD from Stanford.

After completing her PhD, Leslie married an abusive husband, with whom she lived for seven years and had three children. Her marriage ended in the emergency room, where a social worker discovered that her bleeding, bruises, and fractures were a result of being struck by her husband. Her Strategy was to be loyal to people so that they would like her and not leave her. Her Core Pattern was to be an enabler and support people and assist them in whatever they did. Her Shadow Pattern was being a passive-aggressive victim.

Years later, after going through a lot of psychotherapy and moving to India to become a Zen Buddhist and a meditator, Leslie met Jeffrey. She was drawn to his more aggressive and assertive ways of teaching and ended up living with him the last eight years of his life. She revealed to me that he had beaten her constantly to inflict her with suffering for a lack of obedience. He was the cause of her broken fingers, arm, and back. One day, he threw her like a football across the room. She landed on the dining table and broke her back and her right arm. Her dream in life was to write, and yet, she couldn't use her fingers to type. It was clear that she seriously believed Jeffrey loved her unconditionally. She was persuaded that he had the keys to her happiness. She told me that he had helped her transform her anger toward her mom and her ex-husband into compassion. I asked her if Jeffrey was successful in helping her be compassionate toward herself. She replied that he helped her to bypass herself and be compassionate with other people, including him. In a painful act of irony, the book that she wanted to write was about Jeffrey's mastery of healing.

Leslie's pain got right into my chest. I was overwhelmed by the information she was sharing, and I felt guilty that I had not picked up on the fact that she was being physically abused. I wanted to hug her and tell her to please wake up right now. But I kept going with the process. I was awestruck by the extent of her "basic lie" and the impact it had had on her life.

Despite Leslie's awareness of her own Verdict of "I can't do anything on my own" and despite all her spiritual transformation, she was still convinced that her Verdict was true. Her negative thought about herself became a belief that she was attached to, which solidified into a Shadow Pattern that caused her all the suffering. How deeply must she despise herself to allow a teacher to chastise her to this extent? He did not even allow her to go to the emergency room, for fear that he would be arrested. He was asserting her Verdict and reinforcing her Shadow Pattern on a regular basis, using the intimidation techniques to reinforce the idea that she was not capable of being on her own, thinking on her own, or completing any task. Yet in reality, this acclaimed psychic and seemingly compassionate teacher was not able to prepare a meal without her. Even though Jeffrey's psychic abilities may have been unusual, and he may have done many other good things for her or other people, why did Leslie rationalize her silence about his physical abuse? How did she justify granting him a passport to greatness?

Regardless of her intelligence and her maturity in so many areas, Leslie had a big blind spot. She confused her real self with her negative Identity Signature, which prevented her from seeing the truth about herself. Even with all the unbearable suffering she had experienced, she was not able to break free. She was determined to understand his behavior and transform her anger toward her teacher into compassion. She bought into his theories to justify her enabling techniques and to stay attached to a core negative belief about herself that she had obtained early in life from her mother. Completing her PhD, teaching, and accomplishing so much in her life—all of this was totally discounted, in her eyes.

As she was relating her understanding of her teacher/aggressor, Leslie mentioned that Jeffrey's dad had been physically abusive with him, his mother, and his siblings. If I had to guess, I would say that this was Jeffrey's Marker. His Verdict may have been, "I am evil," his Sticker was anger, and his Vessel was his lungs. His Strategy for survival was to be the "psychic healer." He displayed empathy and cried frequently and wanted to be there for others anytime they called him for help. He was compassionate and loving, but like a switch, he could turn on and off his paranoia and become verbally abusive. He was stuck in his neurosis, and despite his abilities, he could not upgrade his internal operating system. He learned to bypass it until his pattern got out of control and his closest students left him one by one, except for Leslie, whose strategy was, "Be an enabler." She thought that his aggression was what she needed to keep her in check.

Their sad story is a perfect example how two Core Patterns can complement each other and at the same time be destructively synergistic: a psychic healer/aggressor met a spiritual victim, and both dramas got deeper and bigger. Their patterns were entangled and reinforced regularly. Neither of them was able to challenge their incorrect perceptions, despite the fact that the healer was teaching healing. He saw unusually clearly into others but was totally blind to his own ailment. It must have been too painful to touch his wounds. His Core Pattern to mask them was that the Healer, and his Shadow Pattern, which he hid from the world and from himself, was the destructive aggressor who believed that he was doing good by inflicting punishment. He believed himself and went deeper in his certainty too far until he reached an unbearable point. In his case, he destroyed himself personally, socially, and physically, until finally, he died a painful death from lung cancer. Yet, as his spirit was leaving this earth, someone held his hands and bowed down to him exactly as he had taught her: his beloved and compassionate victim, Leslie.

It is a tragic or even pathetic image, but this is the nature of human beings when they become entrapped in their false beliefs. This story does not have an entirely happy ending, but it has a wealth of gold to be found in its lessons. Leslie is doing better and is moving forward on her journey to conscious awareness. Her emotional wounds are healing, but she will always carry the physical reminders on her body, like a stigmata.

EXERCISE 8: UNCOVER YOUR SHADOW PATTERN

Please read the exercise thoroughly and write out the questions in your notebook before proceeding.

Open your notebook to your Identity Signature page and review it before you start your breathing and visualization exercise.

Step 1

Sit quietly and move into a state of relaxation. I recommend using the Clear Lagoon visualization we created in chapter two (p. 20). Once you are established there, breathe deeper and deeper.

Step 2

Take yourself back to your Marker event. You are now present to the most painful event of your early life. Stay with it, breathe deeper and deeper, and imagine yourself as the little child you were back then. Stay with the image; let it become clear. Breathe in the fresh air and breathe out the pain. Look at the situation closely; feel it at the deepest level. Let it be. Breathe deeper and deeper.

Step 3

Call upon your child image as you are sitting under the tree by your Clear Lagoon.

Step 4

Call upon the Sticker emotion that is associated with your Marker event. Feel the emotion and the sensation in your body; visualize yourself back there in vivid detail. How old were you? What happened? Why did it happen? Stay with the emotion, let it be, and start breathing again, deeper and deeper.

STEP 5

Recall your Verdict about yourself, the negative statement about the thing you believe you are not enough of. In the case of Leslie, it was: "I am not capable of carrying out any task on my own." Be present to the emotion, the sensation in your body, and your feelings about your Verdict. Leslie felt ashamed all her life. She carried it in the Vessel of her back, and her large hump was very visible. Her emotion was one of deep fear.

Ask yourself the following questions. Ask each question three times and wait for the answer. Pause and breathe in between.

a. Think of someone who you really dislike or despise. *Why do I despise this person? What attributes do I despise the most in him or her? If I am totally honest, between me and myself, have I ever acted in the same way that the person I despise acts? If yes, when was that?*

b. *When was the last time I blew things out of proportion, overreacted, or became unduly annoyed with someone? What was the reason for my annoyance? Have I ever displayed that same the trait that annoyed me? When?*

c. *What are the things I do inadvertently and oftentimes regret after the fact?*

For example, snapping, raising your voice, getting angry, throwing a tantrum, tossing objects, gossiping, and so on.

Is there a common denominator or any similarity among all your above answers? If so, isolate the trait you found. Is it a repetitive negative behavior that could be called a negative pattern? Does it sabotage your relationships at times? Do you regret displaying it sometimes? Is it a Shadow Pattern? Does it represent everything you have avoided to hearing about yourself? Is it connected to your Verdict?

Write down all your answers; your Shadow Pattern should be starting to reveal itself. See if you can summarize it in a few words. For Leslie, her Shadow Pattern was, "I am passive aggressive." She enabled people even when she did not want to, and then she became resentful and would occasionally lash out. Like Leslie, we all have our Shadow Patterns. For instance, my Shadow Pattern is to sabotage myself at times when faced with a crisis.

Step 6

Turn to your Identity Signature page and record your Shadow Pattern, like this:

My name is: Micheline
My Emotional Logo:
    My Marker is: The loss of my father
    My Sticker is: Fear
    My Vessel is: My stomach
My Belief Matrix:
    My Verdict is: I am not capable enough
    My Strategy is: Be super-responsible
    My Proof of Identity is: Stepping into my father's shoes at age nineteen
My Behavior Patterns:
    My Core Pattern is: Superwoman
    My Shadow Pattern is: Self-saboteur

Uncovering your Shadow Pattern is not a pleasant journey, but it is an essential one. I am not suggesting that you will need to dwell in this aspect of your inner space forever, but I strongly recommend acknowledging it and accepting it as a fundamental step in your journey. Many teachers, coaches, and inspirational thought leaders tell us to replace our negative stories with positive ones. If you don't deal with your Shadow Pattern, it will end up dealing with you.

If the Shadow is not recognized and acknowledged, it will come back to haunt us when our guard is down, just as it did in Jeffrey and Leslie's example. It is too easy to turn to spirituality and ignore your painful internal experiences, but this is what some call a "spiritual bypass" that will ultimately disempower you.

On the path of conscious awareness, it is essential that we break through all the layers of our inner selves and get to their source—to look below the surface and acknowledge the deep-rooted beliefs and patterns that run our lives. When we become aware of these—the coping mechanisms that operate our internal systems, our brains, our emotions, and our feelings—then we will be able to disempower them just by noticing them rather than allowing them to disempower us. This is how conscious awareness can free us from even the darkest shadows that lurk in our inner space.

CONNECTING THE DOTS

We have now completed our deep dive and uncovered all the key elements of your Identity Signature: your Emotional Logo, your Belief Matrix, and the Behavior Patterns these gave rise to. The journey is not over, but now you have the knowledge to break the code of conscious awareness and propel yourself into a new level of consciousness. The key to this process is knowing how to recognize the signals that indicate that your past traumas are being activated and being able to connect the dots between your past traumas, your Emotional Logo, your Belief Matrix, your Behavior Patterns, and your actions in the present moment. When you see how all of these things are connected, you can acknowledge the lessons of the past and release them. You can recognize that they are not part of the real you but are instead a part of a *possibility* of you that you have created. Through connecting the dots between your current reactions and your habitual patterns, you can break the cycle of unconsciousness.

In practice, this means paying attention to the present moment, to the arising of negative emotions in response to "triggers"— events that evoke the same trauma as your initial Marker. When you feel a negative emotion about something, you are giving your life a taste of the past. The new incident is a trigger for you to recycle the past story. Recognizing the feeling and the emotion and connecting it to the past trauma can interrupt the cycle and shift your experience in the moment.

In *Working For Good*, author Jeff Klein writes, "Our emotions can be useful monitors of external conditions and barometers for our internal condition, but they do not have to define or control us. By paying attention to them, we can both hear and express the useful messages they convey, and avoid being carried away by them. When we are not aware of what is going on inside ourselves, we are often not aware of how we respond to our circumstances or the effects of our actions on others."[9]

Your triggers and negative emotions are a call to enter the landscape within. When you use the trigger as a portal to self-awareness, then every conflicting emotion becomes an opportunity to look within and ask the question: Why am I feeling this way? Why am I reacting so strongly? What is being triggered right now? Is it a pattern of behavior or a Shadow Pattern? Whichever element of your Identity Signature you can recognize will lead you back to what is operating behind the scenes. Challenging people and incidents become your gifts, as they are reflecting your own emotions back to you and lifting the veil on the deep space within.

In order to be consciously aware, you have to learn to be present, moment-by-moment, to what is happening inside. When you become attuned to your triggers, you start watching for them and using them as real opportunities to evolve your consciousness. Each incident becomes an opportunity to regenerate your essence and realign with its flow. Every moment now embodies the whole process of conscious evolution: the trigger takes you to the inner landscape, and you use it to clear the space and reconnect inside and outside. You use it to heal. Then you can create a new possibility from your deep essence.

This approach may sound self-centered, but in reality, it allows you to be fully present with others, because you are taking the blame and judgment out of the space between the other person and you. You are becoming fully aware of what is at play inside of you, you are attending to your own inner child, and you are not reacting to triggers. Instead, you are recognizing them and using them to dive within and clear the space. You understand what is going on inside you, you notice your own mind and notice the part of you that is aware of the mind, and you create a space between them. It is only then that the part of you that is aware of the mind can connect with the universal mind. Consequently, you become more sensitive to other people's needs. You are no longer projecting your inadequacies, insecurities, and desires for greatness onto others. You understand what is beneath the surface and you see with the naked eye what is happening inside of you and inside other people. Therefore, not only are you able to raise your conscious awareness but you are also naturally able to raise other people's conscious awareness simply through your interactions.

People and circumstances are now your opportunities to choose higher consciousness. Every time you are angry and triggered, it is a new opportunity to dive in, to open up, to liberate beliefs and patterns, to clear the space, to heal, and to swim freely again with power and purpose.

7 STAGE 4: CANCEL YOUR POLARITIES

Know then, proud man, what a paradox you are to yourself.
Be humble, impotent reason! Be silent, feeble nature!
Learn that man infinitely transcends man, hear from your
master your true condition, which is unknown to you.
—Blaise Pascal, *Pensées*

In the introduction, I mentioned that my own journey into conscious awareness began with an unexpected vision that came to me in a moment of crisis. I will share the story of that vision with you now, as it turned out to be the key to the next stage in our dance of conscious awareness.

The year was 1994, and I was living in Montreal with my husband Francois, and our two children. We had recently moved there from Paris, where we had lived for eight years after fleeing Lebanon during the civil war. We loved the multi-ethnic French-speaking culture of our new home, and we easily assimilated. I had started a venture for a financial institution: a brand-new nursing home with an emphasis on Alzheimer's disease. While I was in the process of finalizing the project, Francois was offered a significant career advancement with his company. There was only one problem: he would have to move to Kansas City.

After much debate, we ended up striking a compromise among

ourselves: if my deal did not go through, we would follow Francois to Kansas City. If it did, he would come back to Montreal. Nine months after Francois moved to Kansas City ahead of the family, my deal fell through. Reluctantly, I accepted that the kids and I would soon be moving, again, leaving behind our safe haven and the dream home that we had just finished decorating.

I was no stranger to adversity, and moving yet again brought back many memories of instability. In the midst of it, I had a vivid and powerful dream. I saw two scenes in which I was dealing with my mom. In the first, I was being nice and helping her; in the second, I was angry and hurting her feelings. The two scenes seemed to clash and then neutralize each other—the bad canceled out the good, and a ball of white light emerged out of the friction between the two. I awoke feeling good, but I was puzzled about my dream and its meaning.

The next night, I went to bed and the dream came back, only this time, the scenes featured my father. I saw myself caring for him and loving him before he died, and then I saw myself despising his drinking habit and making unpleasant comments to him about it. Again, the two scenes clashed in front of my eyes, the good canceled the bad, and the light appeared.

These vivid dreams returned every night; they featured a different person each time and two incidents that canceled each other into nothing. I started enjoying my nights. I could not wait to go to bed, as if I had a date with myself. In that state of clarity, it was as if I was looking at myself from the outside, like a movie spectator. I watched the most significant episodes of my life being played back in front of me. I observed the enactment of my virtues and my demons, of that which I wanted to show the world and that which I wanted to hide. Each event carried a heavy weight of being good or bad—a weight that I myself had assigned to it.

My rendezvous with myself lasted a few weeks until one morning, I awoke with no memory of a dream. I wondered if my subconscious was done editing my life stories. Was this "life review" complete? I didn't think there was any important event that had not been displayed in the theater of my dreams during those weeks. I was puzzled by it all. What did it mean? Am I nothing? Is my life nothing? Are all my experiences reduced to nothingness?

My experience was like a riddle that I needed to figure out. In a frenzy, I read books by spiritual authors, studied metaphysical teachings, and went to self-development workshops. Then, all of sudden, I stopped looking for answers; the picture became very clear. I learned great lessons and shed many layers, and finally, my mind connected all the dots.

The vision that I had in my recurring dreams was a powerful metaphor that I did not understand back then. I was only able to decipher it gradually after I went through few more crises of my own. What my dreams revealed was that every decision I had made, at each point in time, had an opposite on the platform of my subconscious. What I came to understand was that I'd been living life from a place of judgment—labeling events, other people, and most importantly, myself as "good" or "bad." When I judged myself as "good," I felt positive and uplifted, and when I judged myself as "bad," I felt heavy and depressed. When the good canceled out the bad in my dreams, I felt liberated from all this polarization and constant judgment. In every dream, at that moment when everything was reduced to zero, the light burst forth. The light was beautiful, warm, and filled me with the deepest love, joy, and peace I have ever experienced. It felt like going home, to my real home. That light was all that was left of me—it was my true self, and the essence of all existence. It was the light of conscious awareness.

The next stage in the Dolphin's DANCE process was born out of my understanding of this strange and unexpected series of dreams. In those nocturnal visions, the good and the bad appeared and canceled each other out. The positive charge canceled the negative one, and the light appeared. The pathway of conscious awareness includes a transcendence of the dualistic "either/or" perspective through canceling the opposition of our polarities.

Until now, the Dolphin's DANCE process has allowed us to delve in and develop our conscious awareness inward. In this next stage, our awakening to what is happening in our inner space becomes a call for action. We will learn how to create a distance between our thoughts and who we really are, how to create a distance between what we believe in and who we are, and how to wake up to the illusion of the false self and its relationship to our Identity Signatures. We will cancel out the negativity from our beliefs and integrate our Shadow Patterns. The boundary between our inner light and the universal light will begin to dissolve and will leave us in a neutral space.

When light is generated from an electrical circuit, the negative and positive charges of electrons and protons connect to create a spark. I can't help thinking that our emotions, through the meaning that we attach to them, are charged, like electrons and protons, positively or negatively. These charges are at the source of our thoughts and beliefs. If we think of a past experience as positive, we feel good about it, and we have positively charged emotions around it, like the protons. In contrast, the negative meanings we attach to past experiences generate negative feelings and emotions, like electrons. Positive charges create happiness, joy, and love, whereas negative charges create fear, anger, or frustration. When we understand that every negative charge has a corresponding positive charge, just as I realized in my dream, we can start transcending the polarity of things and canceling out their emotional charge.

You may ask: If a positive emotion is good, why would I want to cancel it? That's a good question. The answer is that when things are going well and you are feeling positive, there is no need to cancel anything. But when things are going bad and you are feeling caught in negatively charged emotions, you can use their positively charged opposites to cancel them out, which will release you into the "light" of transcendence. Great spiritual masters who have achieved a state of wholeness often don't refer to "good" and "bad" anymore. To them, everything is neutrally charged, but this does not mean that it is boring or meaningless. This kind of neutrality is a powerful spiritual freedom that shines like the light in my dream.

Unlike the great masters, most of us are accustomed to looking at life through a lens of duality. We see opposites as "either/or" rather than realizing that both exist simultaneously and are important. We live in a world of paradoxes that often collide with each other—seeming opposites like day and night, life and death. In reality, death is not the opposite of life; it is the absence of life in that particular form. Once we understand that death and life exist together as part of the same phenomenon, we will be able to transcend the duality of life and death. Everything exists together with its opposite. The two sides of the coin exist simultaneously.

When it comes to us, the same is true. We are good and bad at the same time; we are helpful and selfish, loving and unkind, concurrently. The flaw in our thinking is to consider ourselves "either/or" instead of "both/and." This is why we suppress and avoid "bad" parts of ourselves and try to override them with "good" ones. We tend to focus on one aspect of ourselves and eliminate all other aspects. This is a fallacy in our thought process, through which we become narrow-sighted and can no longer see the whole of who we are. To widen our vision, we need to retrain our neurons to be able to see more than one possibility at the same time. Understanding this "both/and" perspective will allow us to integrate the other parts of ourselves instead of ignoring them and leaving them behind. It is this integration that makes us whole and complete.

The pathway of conscious awareness allows us to include the other side of the coin to the extent that the two sides exist in harmony as part of the whole. The good and the bad become shades of possibilities from the infinite field of potential.

Some people worry that if we transcend good and bad, life will lose its joy and excitement. In fact, the opposite is true. Joy and excitement are not just a result of positive feelings—they are released by tapping into our real essence and the true essence of the others. When we transcend the polarities, we move out of the small boxes of good and bad that our false selves trap us in. We connect with our true selves and discover the joyful peace of existence in the now. Love will occur as a result, and fear will disappear.

This also changes the way we understand God, (or Spirit, Infinite Wisdom, Creator, Supreme Intelligence, and so on). Some traditions insist that "God is good," but in this perspective, we realize that the divine is neither good nor bad; it is beyond our attributes. Divinity exists as a flow, an impulse, a source of life and a force of life.

Consciousness or Universal Awareness is the domain where all undifferentiated possibilities exist together. There is no "good" or "bad" there. Whenever we become aware of a particular possibility, we bring that possibility into existence.

However, a dualistic perspective can sometimes be useful as a tool. When I want to distinguish one option of existence, in order to discern it more clearly, I may have to call on its opposite. From a field of undifferentiated possibilities, all probabilities exist until I differentiate one. At that moment of differentiation when I bring it forward, it becomes alive. So the duality is very useful to create a contrast. This contrast helps us segregate facts and elements that are hard to distinguish or single out. But when we use the dichotomy to judge someone or some part of ourselves, or to eliminate a valid experience or choice, it becomes exclusive. It denies the full experience and becomes a limiting belief.

In this stage of the Dolphin's DANCE process, I will be showing you how to use these principles to release yourself from the biggest limiting belief that holds you back: your Verdict, which is at the source of your Core Pattern. But first, in order to understand this process, let's go back to one of the examples from my recurring dream to see how it might play out with another person.

In one of my dreams, I saw two scenes involving my father. In the first, I was caring for him when he was sick and appreciating how selflessly he had cared for me. In the second, I was frustrated with him because of his tendency to drink too much. Neither of these perspectives contained the full picture. If I look at him and only see his selfless giving, I may have a tendency to judge him positively. If I look at him and only see his drinking, I may have a tendency to judge him negatively. But if I look at him and see all possibilities of existence, I will have a hard time judging or fixing him in any one category. Instead, I will see him in every moment and allow him to be who he is and not limit him to being the person I have created in my mind, based on my judgment of him.

By doing this, I give my dad the opportunity to exist beyond the limitations of his specific actions. I allow his spirit self to occur in the most integrated way possible. This will affect my listening to him, who he is to me, and our relationship together. The possibilities become endless, as we open doors to experience different realities than our preconceived ideas. We get to transform oppositions into complements. The non-opposing realities open the space for the resurgence of what is. We allow reality to appear moment-by-moment without judging it or fitting it into a structure of dualism.

The polarity exists only in the way we perceive reality. We see things as we do, not because that is what is there but because of where we stand. What we see is a function of what we believe in. So what I see may not be the same as what somebody else sees as he or she stands across from me. As for me, what he sees is colored by his experience, his beliefs, and so forth. Our perception is what frames our inner space. We are the creators of our own realities. In this sense, in the example from my dream, I am the creator of who my dad is. I create him according to the possibility that I bring forth about him.

I'm not saying that we should deny the existence of certain facts, or that we should be neutral about whatever happens to us, but by becoming conscious of the meaning we give to an event, we can eventually replace the event itself. This meaning is an assignment of a value to what happened. It is like attributing a grade to a test. When we do this, we limit what can happen to the grade we assign to it. Instead of experiencing it as it is, we experience one aspect of it, the aspect that is given to us by our own meaning, the judgment, and the perception. Our creation determines our experience of the person or/ and the situation. We have trained our minds to think in these terms. And not only do we do this to other people—we do it to ourselves.

We are constantly judging what we are doing and fixating it in the good or bad category. This positive or negative polarity limits our experience of the present moment to its face value. When we do this, we are standing in the way of our own flow. The most powerful example of this was the moment when we judged our Verdict as bad and created a Strategy that we considered "good" to replace it. By doing this, we trapped ourselves in the polarity of the Core Pattern and the Shadow Pattern. If we train ourselves to bring to each quality its opposite, we start canceling our negative feelings toward ourselves and clearing the space within.

This may sound a little simplistic at first, but I ask you not to judge it before you practice it and see what happens. Yes, it is simple—a young child or an elderly person could practice it without any effort. I trained my own mom to practice this at the age of eighty-three, and it changed her life. But it is surprisingly powerful. Ready to dive in?

EXERCISE 9: CANCEL OUT YOUR VERDICT

STEP 1

Open up your notebook to your Identity Signature and read your Verdict.

STEP 2

Sit quietly and move into a state of relaxation. I recommend using the Clear Lagoon visualization we created in chapter two

(p. 20). Once you are established there, breathe deeper and deeper.

STEP 3

Call upon your child image as you are sitting under the tree by your Clear Lagoon.

STEP 4

Imagine your inner child sitting in front of you. Look your inner child in the eye, and ask him or her the following questions:

a. *What is the greatest quality you love about me?*

   Let yourself feel your child's answer, and write it down.

b. *What is the emotion that this quality is generating in you right now?*

c. *What fills your inner space; is it filled with hatred? Love? Is it neutral?*

There are no right or wrong answers; there is only a conscious awareness of what is happening within you.

STEP 5

Turn to a new page in your notebook, and write your Verdict at the top. For example, "I am not worthy," or "I am not lovable," or whatever negative belief arose from your Marker event. Now think of all the examples that prove your Verdict and write them below; leave space between the lines. Write as many examples as you can think of—specific incidents that may involve various people in your life. For example, if your Verdict is "I am not lovable," you might write:

> *I am not lovable to my mom because I yelled at her.*

Or if your Verdict is "I am not worthy," you might write:

> *I am not worthy of my husband because I don't make as much money to contribute to the family as he does.*

Do not stop writing until you have exhausted all examples of you being your Verdict.

STEP 6

Now, go back to the top of your list. In the space below each example, write an example of the opposite, involving the same person or situation. Don't just make up an opinion; dig deep into yourself and find a real example from your life that illustrates the opposite of your Verdict. It does not matter if what you come up with is trivial; all that matters is that it is a genuine example of you being the opposite of your Verdict or making a sincere attempt to do so with the same person. Do not leave any example without writing its antidote underneath. For example:

> *I am not lovable to my mom, because I yelled at her.*
> *I am lovable to my mom, because I hugged her.*

Or:

> *I am not worthy of my husband because I don't make as much money to contribute to the family as he does*

I am worthy of my husband because I work hard to create a beautiful home for our family

STEP 7

Once you are done writing, ask yourself, given the positive statement I have written: Could my negative Verdict be absolutely true? For example, could you be absolutely right about "not being worthy"? If you can't be absolutely sure, then the statement is not absolutely true. Why would you choose to believe something that is not true? Allow the positive statement to cancel out the negative one.

Pause. Take a deep breath. Close your eyes and feel the space present inside of you. Do you still feel that you are your Verdict? Do you still believe that you are not lovable or not worthy? Is it true? And if it is not, why would you choose to live your life based on a false statement? How could you possibly be authentic if you live a life based on an erroneous belief? The "not enough" statements are simply false statements. They fill up your inner space with junk and disconnect you from the Source.

STEP 8

Take a few deep breaths, close your eyes again, and ask yourself the following questions:

a. *Is it possible that I am my Verdict (e.g., not lovable) and its opposite (e.g., lovable) at the same time?*

b. *Is it possible that I am my Verdict (e.g., not lovable) and its opposite (e.g., lovable) and many more things at the same time?*

By doing this exercise, you have taken the negative charge out of your deepest, darkest belief. You can repeat this same exercise for any other strong negative beliefs you have about yourself. When your core negative beliefs about yourself are canceled out, then you will be able to clear your inner space. It is like vacuuming every corner while feeling each feeling and uncovering each emotion carried with the negative belief.

You don't have to worry about finding and canceling every tiny negative belief about yourself, because human beings operate based on the Pareto principle, also known as the 80-20 rule—80 percent of the limiting outcomes in our lives are generated by 20 percent of our negative beliefs. Therefore, targeting the original Verdict has an outsized impact.

AWAKEN TO THE ILLUSION OF THE FALSE SELF

Now that you have liberated yourself from the negative charge attached to your Verdict, you are ready for the most powerful spiritual breakthrough: seeing through the "basic lie" or the illusion of the false self.

Experiencing a major crisis or "dark night of the soul" is not necessary to awaken to the true self, but it is often the way it happens, as it was the case for me. How you relate to the crisis will determine whether it is a transformative event or not.

Let's pause here and look back at the construct of our Identity Signature. This Identity Signature resembles an operating system through which we manifest who we are in the physical world. The minute our Core Pattern fails or our Shadow starts appearing to us, we start doubting who we are since we have equated who we are with our Identity Signature. When the latter fails, it cracks open, and this crack allows the light of awareness to penetrate, which gives us the possibility of a breakthrough to another level of consciousness. It is at this moment that we realize we are not this Identity Signature. We are not this ego. So who are we, really?

For the longest time, I thought that this construct represented who I am. My sense of responsibility was apparent to all, but my motivator was hidden from my own view and from everyone else's view. It certainly helped me succeed for a long time, until one day, I hit a profound crisis and was seriously struggling to resolve it. I became suddenly aware that I was limited in some way, shape, or form. Being "Superwoman" made me responsible for everything and everybody. This came at a heavy cost—a weight that eventually needed to be shed. The worst part was that I had reduced who "I am" to being "responsible for" everything and everybody. I wanted to fix the world. But despite trying very hard, a point came where I could not fix it, and I took this as a failure. The failure cracked my Identity Signature wide open, and I started my process of conscious awareness—my process of moving from the false self, which expressed itself through my Identity Signature, to my real self.

This seminal moment happened in 1996, a couple of years after the series of dreams I described at the beginning of this chapter propelled me to become a seeker. I remember waking one morning in our new home in Kansas City, and despite the spectacular sunrise outside my bedroom window, all I could feel was the pain of a bleeding ulcer, and all I could see was the possible bankruptcy of the healthcare business I'd started after our move. My business was losing money. We had two kids in private schools and parents to support. We could be headed toward a bankruptcy. To me, insolvency was associated with my dad's illness and death. My Verdict of "not being capable enough" was all that I could see. I felt like I was dying. I could not eat, or sleep, or get out of bed.

My faith in myself had gone down the drain. I could not meditate, calm myself down, or step out of the situation. I simply collapsed. I imagined the worst, and the worst was making its way toward me. Nothing made any sense in my life. I could not find the energy or the motivation to play Superwoman anymore. My Strategy collapsed, and so did my sense of self. I was so terrified that I could not get out of my bed. My fear was more crippling than my pain. My meditation and positive affirmations would lift me up a little, but then I would drown down again. I would force myself to think better thoughts and write positive affirmations, but it was just a temporary relief. Why was I unable to shift things more deeply? I wondered. My spiritual practice seemed to treat my symptoms, which made me feel better temporarily, but the source of my ailment was hidden from my view. My anxiety attacks became intolerable.

My gastroenterologist revealed that the cause of my ulcer was a stomach infection due to the presence of a bacteria called H. pylori, which, if not treated, could cause gastric cancer. It dawned on me that my dad, at the very same age, had died from esophageal cancer right after his business crashed. I would have liked to not make the connection; I would have liked to turn the other way, but life was shouting at me, loud and clear. How could I not see the obvious? I started asking myself: Is there a kind of cosmic conspiracy against my father and me? My family? How can I break the cycle?

I knew what I needed to do, but the more I tried to change my thoughts and feelings about my life, the more fearful I became. I was under the impression that I was just tricking myself and manipulating the facts of my life to make myself feel better. It was only when I picked up Louise Hay's breakthrough book *You Can Heal Your Life* that I became clear on the connection between my physical disease and my thought patterns and fear. Louise became my virtual friend; every morning, I would sit in thought with her in my meditation, visualizations, and readings. Her advice was clear: to change my life, I needed to change my thoughts and feelings. But how? The voice in my head was still terrified.

During this period, I also stumbled upon Saint John of the Cross's writings about the "Dark Night of the Soul," which was written in the sixteenth century while the Catholic mystic was imprisoned by the Carmelite brothers who were against his reformation of the Order. He describes the journey of the soul from its materialistic identification to purification of the senses and total union with the spirit. I then moved on to reading contemporary insights from authors like Nancy Napier and Debbie Ford. Slowly, I started understanding that I was living a death of some sort. What died was my ego self, the sense of self that I had been identifying with.

With time, by allowing myself the space to heal, I gained clarity that I had never experienced before. I was afraid of nothing, threatened by nothing. I was able to meditate again. My sense of attachment to the business or to my roles faded away. I started living in the present, connecting to nature and animals. I let go of my attachment to my role as a mother and became a friend to my kids. My old self had literally died, and my true self started to surface. My business stopped being "my" business; instead, it became a labor of love for the whole high-performance and compassionate team that I built around me. We introduced integrative medicine programs at no cost for our residents. In no time, our company was flourishing again, and we became known for the excellence of our quality of care.

What really had collapsed, I would later understand, was the structure of my Identity Signature. I realized that I had bought the business because of my need to prove that I can be successful. I did it in order to make up for my dad's bankruptcy. Now, as I awakened to myself, opened up my Emotional Logo, and started seeing the fallacy of my own limiting beliefs about myself and the limiting beliefs I had acquired and inherited, I leaped into a new level of awareness. The trees started to look greener, the sunsets were more spectacular, and my sense of gratitude and appreciation became deeper. I felt I was pulsating with the breath of life. Every moment became a rebirth to me. My sense of fear vanished totally, and I was feeling a deep connection with everyone and a sense of beauty and love that I had never experienced before.

My experience made it clear to me that something needs to die in us to create space for something else to be born. Death becomes part of a transformation process and not the end. When I changed my beliefs and my patterns, I altered my emotions and my vessel and affected my thoughts I am still the same person with a different outlook on life.

This does not mean that I don't have an ego anymore; it simply means that I am consciously aware of it and can catch its manifestation. Whenever I act out of fear, or from a place of "not enough," or from a compensation strategy to look good and mask my Verdict, I recognize its face. Whenever I compare myself to others or judge others, I know that my ego is occupying the space of my true self. One thing, though, has dissolved forever: the illusion. I do not confuse my Identity Signature with my authentic self. I know that who I am is beyond who I ever think I am.

The literature on these subjects is full of definitions of what is considered a false self and what is considered a true or authentic self, from Freud and Jung to modern psychology to the New Thought movement to contemporary spiritual teachers like Eckhart Tolle, Wayne Dyer, Deepak Chopra, and others. It is not my intention to contrast and compare definitions or to analyze the precise meanings of these often-confusing terms. For me, I simply believe that our Identity Signature represents a false sense of self. When Identity Signatures are confused with who we are, we fall prey to an illusion. A constructed identity has been mistaken for the "self."

To relate this to the work of Freud or Jung, we could say that the Identity Signature is the structure that the ego uses to manifest itself in the world. I like to think of it as a kind of "original sin." The contemporary mystic Eckhart Tolle has a wonderful definition of sin:

> "Sin is a word that has been greatly misunderstood and misinterpreted. Literally translated from the ancient Greek in which the New Testament was written, to sin means to miss the mark, as an archer who misses the target, so to sin means to miss the point ..."[10]

When we confuse who we really are with our identity statements, we do indeed miss the point. We commit this original sin very early in life when we start comparing ourselves to others to measure our self-worth. We start building strong structures of beliefs and patterns of behavior to survive while forgetting our true selves and who we really are. We stray from our essence. It is only when this illusion is challenged that we start realizing the depth of our confusion. To awaken spiritually is to uncover our Identity Signatures and to be present to the illusion that we have created by confusing that Identity Signature with our real selves, which is beyond our Verdicts and the patterns we have created to mask them.

Your Verdict constituted your basic lie about yourself, such as, "I am not capable enough;" "I am not good enough;" "I cannot make it on my own;" or "I am not lovable enough." You rearranged your life to hide your verdict and to show the world a different face. Your Strategy was a decision you made early on, to camouflage the Verdict. Your Strategy served to show the contrary of what you believed you were "not enough" of. Your Core Pattern took a life of its own, and your Shadow Pattern became hidden from your view. You started believing your own act, and so did the people around you as you reenacted your Strategy time and time again and turned it into a Core Pattern. Despite the basic lie of your Verdict being buried deep down, it continued to taint your actions and reactions and created a Shadow Pattern that gets triggered every now and again when your Strategy is proven wrong. You do everything in your power to keep your Shadow Patterns buried deep down—so deep that they become inaccessible to you. You hide them from the world and from yourself; you suppress them, but from time to time, they resurface and create a crisis in your life.

WHO ARE YOU, REALLY?

So, who are you? Are you your body? Are you your emotions? Are you your thoughts? Are you your beliefs? Are you your mental constructs? Are you your psyche? Are you your profession? Are you your experiences? Are you your possessions? Are you your ego? Are you something invisible? Are you really sure that you are all the above?

In these chapters, we have witnessed the limitations of our belief systems, our thoughts, and our behavioral and emotional patterns. We know how ephemeral are our bodies, our looks, and the things we possess or do in life. We have witnessed, through this work, the fallacy of our ego structure. So who are we, really?

One day, when my daughter Jessica was ten, she looked me in the eye and asked, "Mom, what happens if we die and find out that all that we believe in now is not true?"

Well, we don't have to wait till we die to find out—haven't you had that experience a few times in the course of your life? Where you believed something to be the truth and then realized after the fact that your predominant belief was totally erroneous? What if this belief was about who you are?

While it is hard to define who we are, beyond the physicality of our existence, we know that who we are is not reduced to just that, and yet, we live our lives identifying with it. While they do teach us important lessons, our experiences do not define who we are either. They serve to help us learn and to color our perceptions of all future experiences, and they contribute to the formulation of our beliefs. But they are not who we are.

Is there something about us that is more intelligent than the ego, its structure, our possessions, and our actions? Is there something that could be constant, infinite, and permanent? Look at the plants and the birds outside your window, your dog or cat, and the systems inside your body—each made up of countless details orchestrated in a perfectly intelligent system. Is this living force behind all these systems constant? Does it change between yours and mine, between the young child and the old man, the person with a dark skin tone or one with a light one, the CEO or the beggar? Does it differ among the living organisms with which we share the planet? Our ability to grow and change through our cognition certainly separates us from the plants and the animal kingdom. But the force, the impulse behind life, is the same. It is constant, permanent, and supremely intelligent.

Our original self, our authentic self is connected to the Source, to this impulse, to this breath of life. That is who we are, whether we drift, whether we live the illusion, or whether we are awakened. We are plugged into the Source whether we like it or not, whether we choose it or not. So why, then, is it important to become aware of it?

It is important simply because when we are conscious of our Source, it gives us our sense of being. It gives us our sense of purpose beyond our ego structures, beyond our roles. We move into the flow of that which we are becoming and can constantly adjust our dance to the dance of the universe until our dance becomes the dance of the Source. When we are consciously aware, our thoughts, beliefs, and actions start aligning with who we are. We flow at the same rhythm. The waves synch inside of us and outside of us. We become the singer and the song, and we do not question either.

Identifying with the Source is the key to discovering your authentic self and living with joy, love, and creativity. When we become aware of our deep nature and we are conscious of our structures, we eliminate the unnecessary suffering inflicted upon us by our own doing and our conditioning, and we return to the Source of who we are. We become aware of our illusion and become the observer catching ourselves when we fall in the field of darkness and confusion, and we start identifying with our false self. When you first engage in the conscious awareness process, you may realize that you have fallen back into your false self only after the fact, but you will have a choice to bounce back. With time and practice, you will start realizing it sooner, when you feel the urge to react, so that you will have a choice about how you respond and the place you would want to respond from. Falls become less frequent, and bouncing back becomes quicker.

Breaking through the illusion gives us a sense of relief and eases our pain. Of course, it is easier said than done, but conscious awareness gives us access to a state of being that makes us conscious of being plugged into the Source. We recognize that the true self is beyond our human experience, and it is part of the infinite wisdom. Experience, while being necessary and precious, is only one possibility among the field of endless possibilities that we are part of.

This self-awakening brings with it a feeling of myself. When I awoke to my true self, nothing was missing anymore. I stopped identifying myself with more social status, more professional titles, or more tangible assets. I became content with who I am; I accepted all of myself and healed the past. I acknowledged the past as my teacher, looked for its hidden gifts, and accepted its precious lessons.

When you are grounded in your true self, you see yourself as you are. You see yourself without judgment, as neither good nor bad, neither above nor beneath anyone. Instead of reacting to events and people, you can then respond with compassion toward others and yourself, and instead of making fear-based decisions, you can make conscious choices that lead to your own expansion and the expansion of the people around you.

Are you ready to give up your illusion? Then let's dive in. Your inner child may show you the way.

EXERCISE 10: AWAKEN TO THE ILLUSION AND ITS IMPACT

Please read the exercise thoroughly and write the questions in your notebook before proceeding.

Open your notebook to your Identity Signature page and review it before you start your breathing and visualization exercise.

STEP 1

Sit quietly and move into a state of relaxation. I recommend using the Clear Lagoon visualization we created in chapter two (p. 20). Once you are established there, breathe deeper and deeper.

STEP 2

Take yourself back to your Marker event. You are now present to the most painful event of your early life. Stay with it; breathe deeper and deeper.

STEP 3

Call upon your child image as you are sitting under the tree by your Clear Lagoon. Imagine yourself as the little child you were back then. Stay with the image; let it become clear. Breathe in the fresh air and breathe out the pain. Look at the situation closely, feel it at the deepest level. Let it be. Breathe deeper and deeper.

STEP 4

As you are sitting in silence, be present to your Core Pattern in life: "Super Woman/Man," "Victim," "Loving," "Persecutor," "Aggressor," "Helper," "Mr. or Mrs. Fix it," and so on. Ask yourself:

> *What was the impact of being [your Core Pattern] on my life? And on the life of others around me? When did it serve me? When did it impact me negatively?*

Be with the impact. Acknowledge it. Be grateful for what you have accomplished because of it. Thank it and let it go.

STEP 5

Be present to your Shadow Pattern. Ask yourself:

What did my Shadow Pattern cause me to do? How did it impact others? When did it serve me? When did it impact me negatively?

Acknowledge it. Thank it. Let it go.

Step 6

Turn back in your notebook to the page where you worked on Exercise 9: Cancel Your Verdict, and ask yourself:

a. *Do I still believe my Verdict?* If so, notice your attachment to it.

b. *Was I a fair judge with myself throughout my life? Would I want to die having been an unfair judge?*

c. *Who would I be without my Verdict?*

d. *Who would I be without my Patterns?*

e. *Who am I? Am I my body? Am I my emotions? Am I my thoughts? Am I my beliefs? Am I my mental constructs? Am I my psyche? Am I my profession? Am I my possessions? Am I my experiences? Am I my ego? Am I my Identity Signature? Am I something invisible?*

f. Call upon the dolphin in your Clear Lagoon; visualize yourself breathing with him and swimming with him. Describe the similarities between you and him. Describe the differences. Are *the similarities permanent or transient? Are the differences permanent or impermanent?*

Visualize yourself swimming in the clear water with the friendly dolphin. Let go of your attachment to your emotions, your beliefs, your Verdict, your image of yourself, and your Identity Signature. Feel your deepest nature. Connect to it. Connect to the dolphin through your breath, connect to the water, and feel at one with all of this. Stay there as long as you need to.

8 Stage 5: Embrace Your True Self

The wound is the place where the Light enters you.
—Rumi

The fifth and final stage in the Dolphin's DANCE process is about healing the wounds of the past and present and embracing your true self. In the first three stages, we unearthed the various components of your Identity Signature. In the last stage, we experienced the powerful cancelation of the inner polarities, and we saw how this creates space to connect with the light of your true self and allows you to break free of the illusion that you are your Identity Signature. As we moved through these stages, you may have experienced powerful moments of healing simply as a result of bringing the hidden parts of yourself into conscious awareness and acknowledging them. However, there may still be unhealed wounds or blockages, and as long as these remain, you will not be able to fully embrace your true self.

Authentic healing, in this work, is the process of reclaiming your true self from your ego after a major life event, such as a trauma or crisis, either one from your childhood or a more recent one. As we discussed in the previous chapter, often the breakdown of the illusion occurs when we go through a "dark night of the soul." Perhaps it was triggered by a loss, a betrayal, or an unexpected change in circumstances. These moments can be transformative and open up new possibilities, but they are also traumatic and destabilizing. Authentic healing, after a crisis like this, is a conscious return to wholeness and inner peace.

In the shamanic tradition, they call this "soul retrieval." According to Dr. Hank Wesselman and Jill Kuykendall in their book *Spirit Medicine*, soul retrieval is a healing modality that "affords a reunion of dissociated soul part(s) with the person's life essence, thereby allowing individuals to have more of themselves available to live their life in the present moment."[11] You allow yourself to be more of you. Allowing yourself to heal in this way and granting yourself the space to do it helps to rebalance your polarity. You can integrate your shadow and become whole by reconciling with the other aspects of yourself that have been too painful to acknowledge.

This final stage in the DANCE allows you to integrate your whole self. Don't worry if sometimes you feel as if you are going backward—sometimes it is necessary to revisit earlier stages in the process or circle back to integrate what you have learned more deeply. In this chapter, we will explore some of the common obstacles that prevent us from healing, learn how to create a space in which your healing can occur, move beyond the position of victimhood, and engage with the powerful healing work of forgiveness.

Even if you are not initially aware of wounds that need to be healed, don't skip over this stage in the process or be too quick to move on. Just as a runner who falls and injures an ankle must take time to heal and mend the bone before he can run again, we need to allow ourselves time and space to heal inwardly before we can grow and move forward. We cannot just pick ourselves back up immediately after a crisis and get back in the game, any more than the runner can finish a marathon on a broken ankle.

Simply being aware of our wounds is not enough. I have known a few people who were aware of their childhood traumas, conscious of their patterns and shadows, yet seemed to struggle with their own healing. If you don't heal the wounds from the past, they don't vanish; they bleed inside of you. You continue to attract situations that reflect your inner hemorrhaging as you project to the world the vibration of the negative emotion active inside of you. Once you become aware of your wounds, it's essential that you take the time to heal and restore your wholeness. Otherwise, a new crisis could become a new marker in your life. As a result of it, you may develop a new coping strategy that can become a new behavioral pattern.

This process involves more than a simple return to functionality. A major trauma or crisis usually comes associated with a whole web of emotions, feelings, sensations, triggers, and reactions. Becoming whole does not only mean returning to health and well-being, it also involves shedding the parts of this web that do not serve you and aligning back with your Source.

When we hear the word *healing,* it sounds attractive, but in reality, many of us resist it at times in our lives. And we have all watched people we love, at one time or another, become so entrenched in a crisis that they seem unwilling to move through and beyond. There are many complex and often unconscious reasons why we resist the path of healing, so before I share this path with you, let's take a moment to check your willingness to heal. Let's dive in.

EXERCISE 11: WHY CAN'T I HEAL?

Please read the exercise thoroughly and write the questions in your notebook before proceeding.

Open your notebook to your Identity Signature page and review it before you start your breathing and visualization exercise.

STEP 1

Sit quietly and move into a state of relaxation. I recommend using the Clear Lagoon visualization we created in chapter two

(p. 20). Once you are established there, breathe deeper and deeper.

Step 2

Think of a painful event or crisis that you are struggling with right now—a situation that has happened recently and needs healing. You are now present to an event that is painful yet different from the Marker event of your early life. Stay with it; breathe deeper and deeper. Stay with the image; let it become clear. Breathe in the fresh air and breathe out the pain. Look at the situation closely; feel it at the deepest level. Let it be. Breathe deeper and deeper.

Step 3

Call upon your child image as you are sitting under the tree by your Clear Lagoon.

Step 4

As you are sitting in silence, ask yourself the questions below. Ask each one three times while pausing and breathing in between.

   a.   *Why don't I seem to be able to heal this situation?*

   b.   *Is my Verdict the culprit? Am I being blocked by the "not enough" belief that formed as a result of my earliest Marker event?*

   c.   *Is there any other limiting belief in the way of my healing? What is it?*

d. Am I certain that my belief is true, without a shadow of a doubt? How so?

e. Is my belief about why I cannot heal this situation coming from my ego or my true self?

f. What is the pay-off of this condition I am in right now? What is it that I would lose if I were to heal?

g. What would become possible for me and my life if I were to heal?

h. Am I willing to let go of my attachment to my condition?

i. Am I willing to let go of my belief around my healing?

j. Do I really want to heal?

Now that you have answered these questions, it should become obvious to you whether you want to heal or not. You should see more clearly any resistance to healing and be able to let it go. If you feel you are ready to heal and let go, proceed to step five. If not, you may want to put this aside for a day, hold the questions in your awareness but don't force any answers, and then come back and repeat this exercise tomorrow.

STEP 5

Now, picture your inner child totally healed. Close your eyes and stay with this picture. Picture yourself being free of the condition that you need to heal. Exaggerate the outcome of your healing. For example, if you need to heal from a betrayal and regain trust, don't just imagine yourself feeling a little more trusting—imagine yourself writing a book on regaining trust and hugging strangers in the street. Imprint the image in your brain; feel the healing in your body. Exaggerate the emotion. Stay with the emotion. Open your eyes and write it down.

HEALING FROM A CRISIS: FIND ITS GOLD

A major crisis or dark night of the soul is not the only doorway to awaken your inner light, but it is the way it happened to me. It is how we relate to the crisis that will determine whether it will be transformative or not.

Once you have lived through the intensity of the initial crisis and you start to adjust to the new situation in your life, it is important to look for the opportunity hidden within it—to "find its gold." Each crisis is an opportunity for conscious awareness if we learn to step back from it, look for its gold, and learn its lesson.

We have learned through this work that it is not possible to bypass our emotions. How we feel about a situation will get repressed if it is not expressed. Learning how to express our emotions without using them as a weapon to manipulate ourselves or others is a key to nurturing conscious awareness and continuing to fuel our inner light. It is important to hear your inner child and acknowledge his or her pain in order to move through it and not stay stuck in it. Denying a wound will make it seem as if it is not hurting—you can distract or numb yourself with painkillers, drugs, or alcohol, but once the effect of these artificial highs wears off, the pain will resurge and be more intense each time. This often leads to addiction as you seek more potent numbing agents and become more and more dependent on them to manage your crisis for you. While you can deny or numb the pain temporarily, it always reappears at a moment that is not of your choosing, most likely triggered and compounded by another big crisis that may then create the perfect storm.

Through conscious awareness, we can move through the negative emotion of pain and loss and get in touch with our authentic self. There are three common models of dealing with a crisis, which I refer to as the Getting Stuck Model, the Moving Through Model, and the Leap of Consciousness Model.

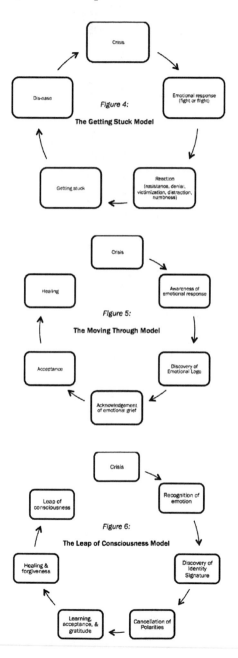

Figure 4:
The Getting Stuck Model

Figure 5:
The Moving Through Model

Figure 6:
The Leap of Consciousness Model

Which of these three models we use to deal with a crisis demonstrates how consciously aware we are. The second model can definitely calm the emotional water and the undercurrent of fear. It will move you through the crisis and may result in learning from it. The third model describes how you can consciously use your crisis to move into conscious awareness. Each time you encounter a crisis, if you practice this model, you will be able to bounce back quicker and quicker and widen your field of consciousness. The quicker you can tune into your emotional guidance system, the more emotionally aware you become, and the more connection to the Source you will experience. The crisis will start to be your playground where you improve your game. The tide of awareness will move you past the grief and the loss and push you into the flow again.

ALLOW YOURSELF A NEUTRAL SPACE TO HEAL

After you go through a major crisis, life transition, or trauma, it is essential to allow yourself time and space for healing to occur. This was one of the biggest lessons I learned after my "dark night of the soul." I needed to give myself permission to take some time with myself and retreat into a neutral space in order to heal.

Once my inner polarities were canceled, the emotions behind the beliefs were annihilated as well. I found myself hanging out in a space of nothingness—a zero-charged emotional state around many of my past major events. It was as if my past feelings had no meanings attached to them any longer. They were neither good nor bad. At first, I was confused and felt as if I had lost my bearings. At the same time, I had a sentiment of inner peace that I had never experienced before. The space within me was empty; it felt like a space of neutrality. Nothing bothered me. I started seeing things more clearly. I even had some episodes of clairvoyance and clairsentience that startled me.

What was most striking about this period in my life was that I discovered that I loved hanging out with myself. Ever since then, I have meditated daily in order to hang out with my true self. I have loved aloneness and never felt lonely. I felt that I had a beautiful presence with me, which I was connected to and flowing with, that resembled the light in my dream. It protected me and was omnipresent. When life got rough, my Clear Lagoon became my refuge. Anytime I needed an answer, I called on my dolphin and his wisdom. The energy of the light helped me deal with the emotional charges, and I was swimming and playing freely again.

Once we recognize our Verdict and our limiting behavioral patterns, we start realizing how we live in a perfect yet dysfunctional osmosis with our environment, based on our illusion. We become aware of how we have surrounded ourselves with people who help us sustain our patterns and enable us to fixate our ego structure. When we choose to suddenly change our game, we could be faced with some resistance from even the closest people to us. They may feel threatened by our change. By altering our behavior, we are indirectly compelling the people around us to adapt and alter theirs. Since they might not be ready to so, they may react negatively and in doing so pull us back into our reactive patterns and affect our transformation process. The concept of retreating to a neutral space can help us to pull back and opt out of the game for a short period of time. It is like a time-out in sports. It allows us to temporary stop and recalibrate. It may take the form of going on a retreat, taking a trip, or just allowing ourselves time alone to disconnect and change.

Creating a neutral inner space like the one I experienced is a powerful arena for healing. It reminds me of the Faraday cage—the enclosure invented in 1836 by scientist Michael Faraday to protect the person inside from electric fields. A Faraday cage works by distributing a steady voltage charge or radiation out through the mesh of the cage that cancels out charges or radiation inside the cage. This image can help you to visualize how you can create a protective shield around you by providing a steady voltage of positive beliefs and emotions to counteract the negative emotions. Your Faraday cage is a metaphor for giving yourself the space to transition into that which you are becoming after the crisis, while blocking the negative interference of the environment around you. It allows you a safe place to honor the past and its lessons.

I am not suggesting that you should always live behind this shield, but it will provide you with a temporary safe space in which to experience your process of healing. What I recommend is that you create your Faraday cage after a major transition and spend time there in your own neutral company to allow your feelings, emotions, and thoughts to heal. After a major setback, I sometimes take a few days to be in silence, with just a lit candle and a little food and water, and engage in deep contemplation and meditation. Some people call it recharging their batteries, but I call it neutralizing my batteries. However, if you fall short of canceling the negative charges and find yourself judging, be kind to yourself. When your child falls, do you beat him up or hug him? Why would you deny yourself self-love when *you* fall?

By neutralizing the charges with love and kindness, we are clearing our own space and making ourselves available to ignite our own light from the universal light. Hanging out in this safe space temporarily is not an excuse not to act, but it is a place of acceptance and gratitude. It is a way of allowing your deep connection with the universe to emerge. Every time you go through a major crisis or a setback, you die to who you have been—you no longer are who you were, but you are in transition. You don't yet know who you are becoming. This phase should be respected and not rushed through, so you can allow yourself to heal and assimilate the lessons.

You also need to allow space and time for your biological state to align to your new emotional state, which opened up your awareness. After my recurring dreams, I had bouts of unexplained dizziness for months. Looking back, I can understand that my body needed time to adjust to my new state of conscious awareness.

Every time I go through a major crisis or I fall short of my expectations, I go to my Clear Lagoon and retreat into silence. When I feel I need more time to heal, I give myself permission to go to my Faraday Cage. I envision a protective shield around me, behind which I can cancel my emotional charges, rebalance my own polarity, and reconnect to the light. While hanging out in my own company, I take time to appreciate myself and the lessons that I have learned. This is my time for gratitude. Once I feel that my inner space is clear, I see myself blossoming from the crisis. I imagine my favorite flower, the lotus, and remind myself that it was born from the mud. I thank the universe for its lessons.

While the Faraday Cage is important as a place to rebalance your energy when something has broken down in your life and you have not broken through it yet, there is a danger in staying in the cage too long. You can isolate yourself and build a barrier from the flow. It can shield you from the positive energy that is necessary to rebuild you up and propel you forward. As long as you are allowing the positive energy in and using it to cancel out the negativity, you will be fine. The pitfall is that you can become reclusive and shield yourself in a way that you don't allow the positive in. In that case, you would be building barriers shielding you from your own purpose, from love, and from your potential for growth and development. It is easy to be in harmony when you are a reclusive monk; it is much harder to keep that harmony when you are facing adversity in the world, so you need to remember to get out and practice outside that cage. If you stay attuned to your inner space, you will feel the nudge of the universal impulse to move forward, which will let you know when your healing work is done.

FORGIVE THE UNFORGIVABLE

One of the most important aspects of healing is forgiveness, particularly when your crisis has been caused by a betrayal. Betrayal comes as a shock, a harsh reality that violates your deepest trust. Sometimes the shock can numb us, and we don't even move immediately into a fight-or-flight response. We become paralyzed by devastation and disbelief. Once we do begin to react, it's normal to feel anger, sadness, humiliation, and a desire to retaliate.

In order to heal from betrayal, it is essential to learn to forgive. Sometimes people think of forgiveness as a favor that they render to the person who betrayed them, and this often prevents them from doing so. They think it will be letting the other person off the hook or condoning his or her behavior. In reality, forgiving is an act of kindness toward oneself. Forgiving is not excusing the behavior of the other; it is removing the negative charge from your emotional experience so you can heal your heart and master your circumstances. Forgiveness is not only about having compassion toward the other; it is having compassion toward yourself.

If you decide not to forgive or feel you can't forgive, you are simply giving your power to someone else in addition to dealing with a loss or an open wound. Hurting, grieving, and processing are natural steps that need to be acknowledged and accepted. Allowing yourself to be angry and move through all the stages of loss and grief is healthy and necessary. Staying stuck in loss and grief will just make you more bitter and stop your flow of consciousness.

A TALE OF TWO BETRAYALS

Maria and Cecile are two women I know who both experienced the betrayal of a cheating husband. Both were shocked, devastated, humiliated, and angry, and both divorced their husbands. Yet each of them moved through her experience in very different ways. Comparing their stories illustrates the power of forgiveness.

Maria was our housekeeper for a long time. Her husband, Pedro, cheated on her early in their marriage. Maria only discovered her husband's infidelity seven years later, when she received a call from his mistress confessing their affair. After her initial devastation and disbelief, she went up to her husband's closet and packed all his belongings in black trash bags. When Pedro came back home, she confronted him about his affair and asked him to take his belongings and to leave the house right away and never come back. Shocked and humiliated in front of his family, he took the black trash bags and left with his head down. She didn't even allow him to say good-bye to their only son.

Maria divorced Pedro and was able to get full custody of her little boy. Slowly but surely, she regained her ability to function normally. She had the full support of her clients, as she was excellent at her job. Unfortunately for her, Maria had no foundation upon which her feelings could heal. She kept suppressing her emotions, telling the story of her ex-husband's betrayal to whomever she met and deploring her bad luck. She began to date again, but she developed a new post-crisis Verdict: "I am not woman enough," and a new Strategy: "Never again will I trust any man in my life." She became bitter and ended up breaking other men's hearts to avoid being hurt.

At one point, I raised the topic of forgiveness with Maria. She just laughed and declared, "Maria does not forgive!" I discovered that she had learned this attitude very early in life, when her grandmother left her grandfather after discovering that he was unfaithful. Her family rallied around her grandmother, and she had never seen her grandpa since. Continuing this tradition, Maria did not forgive her husband. More importantly, though: she also did not forgive herself.

Maria became convinced she was a victim of her circumstances, and in doing so, she gave all the power to her ex and could not claim it back. She kept repeating, "I was faithful to him and loved him with all my heart; why did he do this to me?" The truth was that Maria was not responsible for what Pedro did. She did not make him cheat or lie—these were his own choices. Her only mistake had been to trust him. But even when she stopped trusting him, she gave him full power over her life by not letting go of her grudge toward him and forgiving him. Remember Maria's story as I tell the story of another couple, Cecile and Mark.

A close friend of mine, Pierre, who is a life coach, was working with this couple, and he asked me to join him in guiding them through a three-day coaching workshop to design the next chapter of their lives. Cecile, a teacher, and Mark, a surgeon, had been married for almost two decades; their son was in college, and they had recently become empty nesters. I was touched by the kindness of this couple and their willingness to consciously create a common future, although they didn't seem to me like a couple who were in need of counseling.

The last part of the workshop was about creating a life of TAI, which stands for Transparency, Authenticity, and Integrity. This section of the work was very powerful. Pierre asked Cecile and Mark to look back at their life and describe what these values meant to them. To our surprise, Mark left the room and took off. He did not answer his phone, and we were all concerned. Two hours later, he returned, but his demeanor had changed. His face was severe and his brows furrowed in sadness and anger. He came in, sat down on the couch, and without any warning, asked Cecile for a divorce.

We were all shocked. It came out of nowhere. Cecile had no idea why this was happening and begged Mark to explain. "I am making this decision for you," he replied, "because you are better off without me. You deserve better." Then he closed down again, and it took Pierre a few more hours to crack open Mark's shell and to get him to tell the truth. Mark had been cheating on Cecile for eighteen years, with many women. Cecile looked stunned and tears welled up in her eyes. She tried to speak but could not. We stopped the workshop, and Pierre took Cecile on a walk. I stayed behind with Mark, who was clearly relieved at having finally told the truth, however painful it was. Pierre told me later that the couple had divorced and Cecile was continuing to work with him.

A couple of years later, I participated in another workshop that Pierre had created called "Mastery of Circumstances." Both Cecile and Mark participated in the seminar. For me, the most powerful aspect of the workshop was observing how these two people had moved through their difficult circumstances.

While Mark had not yet fully taken responsibility for his actions, and he regretted his divorce, practicing the values of Transparency, Authenticity, and Integrity certainly put him on the right track. Cecile, on the other hand, was strikingly changed. Her joy was contagious, the stories she shared were inspiring, and her beauty was dazzling. At one point, she spoke to the group about what she had been through and how it had changed her.

"Before I knew that Mark cheated on me, I felt that I was a very special woman. I felt superior to others. Today, I feel that I am like every other woman in the world. I am no better and no worse. I am like the beauty pageant winner, the call girl, the queen, the maid. I have no ego left here to protect me; I am vulnerable.

"I can only live in the present. The past hurts too much, and I do not want to project it onto my future. I am leaving it behind. I am grateful—I had a good life and raised a beautiful son. I am grateful to Mark; without him, I would not have my son. He was a loving and responsible father and a good provider. Above all, I am grateful to Mark for my freedom today. I don't need crutches. I am on my own and enjoying every minute of it. The wound that was created inside of me is deep and bloody. One thing I am sure of is that it will always hurt when I visit this wound, but I have no intention of making it my dwelling. I cried myself out. I forgave Mark, and most importantly, I forgave myself. I will never excuse Mark for lying to me or cheating on me. I will never excuse him leaving me alone for nights at a time pretending that he was at work, but I forgive him because he did not know better. I forgive myself for not realizing what was going on because I did not know better. I don't hold on to things I can't change. I accept the hand I was dealt, and I am grateful today that I don't need an emotional crutch to lean on. I have developed emotional resilience out of this crisis."

Cecile was and still is my example of forgiveness. I was in awe of who she had become, and I sincerely don't know if I could have handled this type of situation the way she did. What I did know without a doubt was that she gave me a real-life example of what forgiveness and love look like, and I was honored to participate in her journey. She could have done what Maria did—refuse to forgive, withdraw her trust from all men, and live in bitter and lonely isolation. Instead, she chose the healing path. She used this tremendous crisis in her life to move into healing and into conscious awareness. Her own Transparency, Authenticity, and Integrity helped her to reestablish her trust in herself. Eventually, she became a published and well-known author in Quebec, and she is now leading workshops for couples.

These two stories show the dramatic difference that forgiveness can make. Again, I am not saying you should try to jump to forgiveness before all your feelings of grief, anger, or betrayal have been worked through. That would not be real forgiveness—it would be a bypass to try and avoid the hurt. Declaring a premature forgiveness while the wound is still bleeding is just a Band-Aid, not a healed skin.

A hurting heart is a vulnerable heart; it is a window into opening up your emotions and moving through them. This is why it is important to grieve after a crisis and to allow yourself to feel the feelings without judging them. It is essential to let your emotions arise. When these crucial moments happen, it is hard not to identify with the feelings. It takes a lot of mindfulness and conscious awareness not to. Ideally, we want to let the feelings surface and detach from them as the observer of what is happening. Only then can we feel the sorrow and the joy at the same time, feel the pain and realize that we are not the pain, cry but know that there is this internal peace that no one or nothing can disturb.

To work through the hurt and feelings is not an easy task; it takes courage, perseverance, and self-awareness. You cannot detach from the pain and suffering as long as you are giving a meaning to the suffering that you are identifying with. For example, Maria had created the meaning "I am not woman enough." Cecile admitted that she, too, identified with that meaning for a while. What

happened to her made her feel inferior to other women at first. Bu.
when she let go of that interpretation, she realized that none of us
are special. Indeed, in the eyes of the divine, we are each unique,
but we are not more or less than the other. Through extensive
coaching with Pierre, Cecile worked through her feelings and was
able to dive in and liberate her emotions. She became conscious of
her beliefs and recognized that Mark did not cheat to hurt her; he
cheated from another place of "not enough" for himself as well. He
cheated from a place where he felt inferior and was always looking
for more to make him whole. This did not excuse his actions—
Mark could have chosen another behavioral pathway that would
have taken into consideration Cecile, his family, and his marriage.

One of the most important steps on the healing path is to
forgive yourself before forgiving anyone else, for the simple reason
that you can't truly forgive the other if you have not experienced
forgiveness toward yourself. It is always important to recognize
your responsibility in whatever is happening in your life, but it's
equally important not to confuse this with feeling guilty about it.
Dealing with self-blame, humiliation, and at times, self-loathing,
is inevitable on the path of self-forgiveness. Even Maria, who
blamed her husband very vocally for what happened, secretly
blamed herself for not being enough. She was immobilized by
this feeling and could not move past it. Cecile discovered in her
process of forgiveness that she felt guilty for not having picked up
on Mark's cheating earlier, and for denying and suppressing her
own suspicions and discomfort. She struggled with the fact that her
intuition had betrayed her, or perhaps she had simply not listened to
it. The biggest step on her path of forgiveness and healing was for
Cecile to be able to make peace with herself, to accept her denial,
to accept that she had silenced her intuition, to accept that she had
turned a blind eye, and to come to grips with her role as an enabler.

When Cecile was able to confront this dark shadow, make
peace with it, and forgive herself, she was able to move through
her crisis, release the judgment about herself, and then move on

to forgive Mark for the unforgivable. By doing so, Cecile moved up her conscious awareness to a different level. She uncluttered her inner space, as well as the space between Mark and her, which allowed them to continue to co-parent their son without conflict and tension. As a result, she opened up her inner space for the universal energy to heal her and allowed it to flow through her with ease, gratitude, love, and compassion. Her crisis was the best gift of her life.

What makes these stories interesting is that in both cases, the practical outcome was the same—both couples divorced. But the two women were in radically different states of consciousness. Forgiveness is really about you; it does not matter what happens to the other person. If you accept what happened and you acknowledge its lessons, as Cecile did, you will start moving through your loss and grief. Letting go of what happened will be a natural result, and forgiveness becomes your desirable outcome.

On the other hand, if you keep regurgitating the story to every newcomer in your life, as Maria did, you will get stuck. You will create a pattern of thoughts that gets fixated permanently. The crisis will become the magnet of your life and attract more of the same negative outcomes. Like attracts like—this is the basis of the law of attraction. If you dwell in loss, bitterness, and grief, you will attract more loss, bitterness, and grief. You will also attract negative and critical friends, since misery loves company, which in turn will reinforce your miserable experience and keep it alive. If you decide to work toward forgiveness, you will feel compassion and love. Your positive attitude will attract and create situations and events that will match your positive outlook and expectations. You will attract and manifest love and compassion in your life.

So, are you willing to move past grief and loss? Are you ready to forgive? Let's dive in.

EXERCISE 12: ARE YOU WILLING TO FORGIVE?

Please read the exercise thoroughly and write the questions in your notebook before proceeding.

Open your notebook to your Identity Signature page and review it before you start your breathing and visualization exercise.

STEP 1

Sit quietly and move into a state of relaxation using the Clear Lagoon visualization we created in chapter two (p. 20). Once you are established there, breathe deeper and deeper.

STEP 2

Call upon your child image as you are sitting under the tree by your Clear Lagoon.

STEP 3

As you are sitting in silence, think of somebody in your life who betrayed you and whom you have not forgiven yet. Remember the incident, the shock, the pain, and the anger that the betrayal has caused.

STEP 4

Breathe deeply, turn to your inner child, and ask him or her:

a. *What are you feeling right now about the betrayal? Are you angry, devastated, grieving, appalled?*

b. *What are you feeling about the person who betrayed you? Do you miss him? Do you miss your relationship with her? Do you despise him?*

c. *What are you telling yourself about what has happened? Are you humiliated or ashamed? Do you feel stupid to have trusted? Do you think you're naïve or gullible?*

Honor the feelings and be compassionate with your inner child. Let her express her feelings, her anger, and her grief.

STEP 5

Think about all the happy moments that you had with the person who betrayed you. Think about the positive qualities that you admired in that person. Acknowledge them, honor them, thank them, and let them go.

STEP 6

Knowing that like thoughts attract like experiences, what thoughts, signals, and vibrations are you putting out into the universe about yourself? Do you think these thoughts are related to your Identity Signature? Are you willing to let go of these thoughts?

STEP 7

Think about the negative thoughts that you are having right now as a result of the betrayal, for example: "I am not lovable." Think of an instance of your life demonstrating the opposite of this Verdict. Affirm the opposite to your inner child: "I am lovable and I love myself."

Step 8

Think about the person who betrayed you. Do you think he or she was operating from his or her Identity Signature?

Step 9

Start breathing slowly and deeply again. Picture the other person standing facing you. Picture a cord linking both of you through the navel, like an umbilical cord. Very gently, take the hand of the other person. With your other hand, cut the cord. Tell the person: I forgive you and release you. Send him or her compassion, and let go.

As soon as you send compassion and release the person, you will feel lighter. You may feel a surge of love and compassion toward yourself. The new positive vibration that you are putting out into the universe will become a new pattern of positive emotions, and as long as you believe and reaffirm your positive belief about yourself, you will start attracting positive people and circumstances in your life and rebuilding your own trust.

Step 10

As you breathe deeply, visualize hugging your child. Let the child be; let yourself be. Visualize a bright, golden light coming through your head and cleansing you, cleansing your inner child. See all your organs being enveloped by the light. Breathe deeply and let go of all the anger as you exhale.

MOVE FROM VICTIM TO MASTER OF YOUR CIRCUMSTANCES

The most critical shift in changing your level of awareness is stepping out of being a victim of people and circumstances and learning to accept people and circumstances for what they are. The next step is to look inside yourself—not as blame or self-criticism but as an acceptance of your accountability in the matter at hand.

Whenever a crisis hits, our first response is "fight or flight." This is an adaptive response that human beings developed very early in our evolution. We learned to react to any threat of danger in this way, and this pattern of response became imprinted in the oldest part of our brains, which neuroscientist Paul D. MacLean called the "reptilian brain." This ancient structure is responsible mostly for unconscious and instinctive responses. There are other parts of our brains that developed later, like the mammalian brain, where feelings like love, joy, pleasure, anger, grief, and so on reside, and the primate brain, where data is processed through rational consideration and conscious strategic planning. But when a threat occurs, the reptilian brain tends to take over, and we respond instinctively.

When we are operating instinctively, reacting in "fight or flight" mode, we tend to blame others or a circumstance for what is happening to us, and therefore, we feel victimized by events. In victim consciousness, there is no possibility for healing. As long as we feel like victims, we will only dwell in self-pity and try to get people to sympathize with us. We will revisit our traumas over and over again as we try to use them to get attention from others.

Because humans are meaning-creating beings, we soon start creating a mountain of meanings around what has happened to us. At times, we may even forget what happened but still harbor the meanings, the grudges, and the feelings of "poor me." When we behave like victims of events, people, or circumstances, we become cut off from our own inner self. Life becomes a jail we cannot seem to escape from, and healing is not even a consideration.

No matter how horrible the events of your life may be, if you are not able to shift your consciousness from victimhood to mastery, you will not be able to get out of the jail and reclaim your true self. It takes tremendous strength and courage to make this shift—especially in the midst of very challenging situations. If you are dealing with a major crisis, such as the loss of a loved one, a betrayal by someone you trusted, or an unexpected health crisis, it is natural that you would be asking yourself, why me? But if you dwell there too long, you will come to believe in your victimhood, and then you won't be able to get out of it. Moving beyond victimhood is about moving out of the reptilian brain into our more evolved, rational primate brains, and shifting into mastery of your circumstances by bringing more conscious awareness to your inner space. The brain is the physical structure through which consciousness is organized; without it, we don't have a mind. You can learn how to silence the primitive, unconscious reptilian brain when you don't need it for survival and activate the cortical or primate brain to connect to conscious awareness.

The first self-help book I read, back when I was seventeen years old, was Dale Carnegie's *How to Stop Worrying and Start Living.* I picked it up about a year after my dad died, during my freshman year in college when I started suffering from bouts of crippling anxiety. What I loved in his book was the suggestion that in each crisis, you should ask yourself the question: What is the worst that can happen to me now? Once you have the answer, you should work on accepting the worst and then make a plan to improve on it. I applied this method all my life and it worked for me.

The tools we have used so far in this book are designed to help you achieve the mastery. Your Emotional Logo, for example, will serve as a guidance system. Being able to acknowledge our emotions in moments like this—I am frightened, I am hurting, I am angry, I am ashamed, and so on—is an essential step. Only when our emotions are dealt with can we move to acceptance with sincerity. Too often, we deny ourselves the opportunity to grieve and feel the pain, and thus, we deny ourselves the possibility of full healing. We deny our injury and try to bypass our emotional self, our mammalian brain, by ignoring it. We deny our emotional self the space that it is entitled to, and thus, our healing will remain partial and our emotions will have to find a way to express themselves through different avenues, often with unhealthy consequences.

Once you have identified and acknowledged the emotions associated with a particular event, it is important to ask yourself whether your ego is at play. The way to discern the ego's involvement is to check and see if the original Verdict is present. Does this crisis make me feel "not enough"? If so, it will be helpful to link your present feeling to the emotion of your Emotional Logo. This will heighten your awareness and make you realize that despite it being a new event in your life, you are reacting to it according to your past patterns of thoughts and behavior. In reality, you are not living a present-moment event but rather reliving an old event from the past repackaging itself as a new occurrence. It is like receiving an old gift wrapped up in new wrapping paper.

Once you have given your emotional self the space to be acknowledged and heard, then you will be able to move toward accepting your circumstances. You can't change the circumstances of what has already happened, but you can shift your attitudes toward them. The crisis will inevitably have closed doors that you were familiar with and opened doors to the unknown that you are unfamiliar with and may be afraid of. Accepting what is at its face value, without scaring yourself by obsessing over "what ifs," is a key to moving from victimhood to mastery.

In any situation, if you want to move beyond victimhood, you will need to turn the mirror toward yourself and find the ways in which you may be responsible for the suffering you are in. This doesn't mean you should blame yourself for things other people have done to you, but rather that you should sincerely look to see if there are aspects of the situation for which you can take responsibility. For example, in unfortunate events like the loss of a job or a crisis with a sibling, it's important to have the courage to ask yourself: What is my responsibility for creating this in my life? In the event of the death of a loved one, if you feel that once you have moved through the stages of grief, you are still stuck and cannot move on, the question becomes: What is my responsibility for creating this attitude toward the loss? Negative emotions can become addictive; they can give us an excuse for not acting and can also, through repetition, become a vibrational pattern of thoughts and behavior.

When I say you should accept what is, I don't mean you should not attempt to do anything about the difficult circumstances in your life. On the contrary, when you accept what is handed to you, you can weigh the situation logically and come up with a conscious plan of action by using your upper primate brain where your rational capacities live. If you resist, you remain in the reptilian brain and its reactivity. Whenever you are peaceful, your actions will come from peacefulness and trust in yourself.

Accepting what is handed to us is not always easy, but resisting it makes the negative feelings persist. If, on the other hand, we can let it be without resistance, we allow the universe to unfold its bigger plan, which we can't possibly see from where we stand at the time of crisis. The crisis we are in may become the best gift of our lives.

My close friend Karl constantly reminds me that once you are in a situation, you have only two choices: resisting it, fighting it, and becoming miserable, or accepting it and shifting your attitude toward it. Karl put this wisdom into practice last summer, when he was diagnosed with throat cancer. He is a healthy, athletic man in his early fifties, so it came as a shock to him when the tumor was discovered. He had to go through chemotherapy and radiation therapy. As a result, he could not eat or speak for almost nine months. He lived alone, and at times he was scared to spend the night by himself; the pain medication caused him to hallucinate. Karl was a business consultant, but he was not able to concentrate on his work. He lost his consulting contracts and spent his last pennies paying for his medical bills. He had to give up his beautiful home and his car and move to a low-income residence.

Yet when I talked to him about his losses, he said, "Cancer was the biggest gift of my life." He proceeded to tell me about the realms of consciousness he touched. His views on life and death changed totally. The kindness that he encountered during his sickness, even from complete strangers, made him believe that he was loved by everyone and by the universe. Having been more of a mental person, he now opened himself up to experience love as energy. "If someone told me today that I could go back and live the last year again without the experience of cancer, I would refuse," he said. Through losing everything in his life, Karl gained himself. He opened his heart, accessed his intuition, discovered the world of energy and healing, gained access to the Source, tasted unconditional love, and he leaped into "a new realm of consciousness"—the title of a workshop he has created to share his insights with others. What a gift he is for me and for humanity.

Releasing yourself from victimhood is a critical precursor to healing and to flourishing, as Karl did. Just as positive thoughts and positive feelings can promote spiritual and physical healing, negative thoughts and negative emotions like victimization, resentment, anger, and frustration are equally powerful in preventing mental and physical healing.

Heal your beliefs; doing so will heal your life. Indeed, if you look at all the struggles you have right now in your life and examine them, you will find that behind each one of them, there is a self-limiting belief. Your struggles may be relational, financial, and health- or career-related. I am not saying these struggles are not real, or that your beliefs caused the problems in the first place. It is very unfortunate that you have found yourself in the particular circumstance you are struggling with, and it is perfectly normal and understandable to feel devastated, frustrated, angry, and vulnerable. Yet once you have had time to move past the initial trauma, if you find that you are still stuck in patterns that seem to keep recurring in your life, then you need to turn your attention away from the external circumstances that you are blaming and examine your beliefs instead.

In order to move from victimhood to mastery of your

circumstances, you have to appreciate the lessons you have learned from the situation and heal the wound that was created as a result. If we don't heal our recent wounds, every time we have a new crisis, they will resurface and infect the new ones, which will retrigger our emotional signature.

So, are you willing to move through your crisis and master your circumstances? Let's dive in.

EXERCISE 13: ARE YOU A VICTIM?

Please read the exercise thoroughly and write the questions in your notebook before proceeding.

Open your notebook to your Identity Signature page and review it before you start your breathing and visualization exercise.

STEP 1

Sit quietly and move into a state of relaxation using the Clear Lagoon visualization we created in chapter two (p. 20). Once you are established there, breathe deeper and deeper.

STEP 2

Call upon your child image as you are sitting under the tree by your Clear Lagoon.

STEP 3

As you are sitting in silence, think of the most recent crisis in your life that shook you profoundly and cracked your heart wide open—a circumstance that caused you pain and suffering and created a deep wound inside of you. Breathe deeply, turn to your inner child, and ask the following question:

Where did I let you down, and how?

Then ask yourself:

*If I had to relive the situation, would I live it differently?
If yes, in what way?*

STEP 4

Be present to the impact of the crisis in your life. List any positive effects that occurred as a result of it. For example, it could have given you the power to cope with adversity; it could have taught you an important lesson; it could have brought you closer to someone in your life; it could have given you access to a new level of consciousness. List any positive gains.

STEP 5

Knowing that the two choices available to you are to accept or resist the crisis, choose to accept it. Release your resentment to the universe, and thank it for the gold it gave you through the lesson you learned from it. Most of the time, the learning and the gold do not appear until after you go through the crisis.

STEP 6

Start breathing slowly and deeply again. Reassure your inner child that you are looking after and protecting him or her. Let go of the feeling of hurt and replace it with infinite gratitude.

STEP 7

Visualize your wound, close it with your hands, caress it, thank it for its lessons, and release it to the universe. Picture yourself opening your hands to receive the gifts from the universe, and thank the crisis for its gold. If you don't see the gold yet, just thank the universe for the gift coming your way as you are going through the crisis.

STEP 8

Replace the scar with a lotus flower—the flower that grows from the mud—as a beautiful reminder to share your valuable lesson with people who are going through similar crises.

RECONNECT YOUR INNER LIGHT TO THE UNIVERSAL LIGHT

Let's go back to the vision in my dreams for a moment. After the polarity was canceled, the light appeared. It was the most beautiful light that I had seen in my life. I was watching a festival of light, and at the same time, I was experiencing its warmth flooding through me. I merged with the light. I became it. It became me.

I realized that the light was a power much greater than me, yet I was connected to it. It became clear to me over time that the way I connected to the light was through my focused awareness around my thoughts, my beliefs, and emotions. Only when the space within me was cleared out of my negative thoughts, beliefs, and emotions was I able to invite and receive the light. By making space within, I became a lightning rod for the Source light, which gave rise to an inner peace and a deep attitude of gratitude toward each and every experience I had. My past became a collection of opportunities that pushed me toward greatness. My life stopped being mine but rather became a shared experience with the Source.

Light and fire has been a symbol of the Source for millennia, which is why candles and fires are used in ceremonies of worship in multiple religions and cultures. From Christian services to Pagan rituals to Jewish rites to Hindu ceremonies, the light is a symbol of the joy and life -giving power of the Source.

The light in my dream represented the Source, and my own connection to that light represented my true self, which is like the spark of the Source in each individual human being. When we align our inner self to the light, we become the extension of the Source itself. In the same way that we are longing to connect to Source energy, Source energy is longing to connect to us. Before we came to our bodies, we were pure consciousness; when our bodies die, we go back to pure consciousness. So why do we need to be consciously aware in the brief time we are embodied on earth? I believe it is because through our conscious awareness, we are allowing the spirit to have a human experience. The French Jesuit mystic and philosopher Pierre Teilhard de Chardin said, "We are not human beings having a spiritual experience; we are spiritual beings having a human experience."[12]

If we fill in our human experience with junk, we are preventing the flow of spirit. We clutter our capacity to perceive and receive spiritual possibilities. We end up living the human experience only partially. On the other hand, if we allow spirit to have this human experience fully, the interaction between the spiritual and human fields could bring about infinite possibilities of conscious existence. Our human and spiritual nature will be dancing harmoniously to the same rhythm. They will be singing the same song. They will be contributing consciously to the universal consciousness.

PART III

LIVING WITH
CONSCIOUS
AWARENESS

9 Conscious Awareness On the Go

The whole point of being alive is to evolve into the
complete person you were intended to be.
—Oprah Winfrey

Congratulations on completing the Dolphin's DANCE process of conscious awareness. Does this mean your journey is over, and you will never stumble or fall down again? Of course not! No matter how long you've been on a path of growth, you will, from time to time, get stuck in unconscious patterns that don't serve you—or anyone else, for that matter! When you get triggered in this way, your Patterns take over, you start identifying with your negative thoughts, and your energy and passion dip. When this happens, the most important thing is just to acknowledge it and accept it, and then reapply the process of conscious awareness. In this chapter, I'll be teaching you a simplified version of the process that you can practice "on the go." I call it the Quickstep DANCE.

Before you can use this process, you have to be willing to acknowledge whatever issue has arisen. You cannot deal with what you don't acknowledge. To acknowledge something is to admit its existence. It is to be able to recognize it as valid and having power over you. Once you do this, you need to be kind to yourself instead of judging or having a negative opinion about the fact that you took a dip. When you are consciously aware, you don't have to be perfect. Since the false self is intermingled with our higher self, it is only natural to fall at times during our journey. You are in a dance with the universe, a constant movement. But when you stumble, you do have a sacred responsibility to reinstate your consciousness and reenter into being authentic. You have the obligation to become the observer of the I and notice when you are out of integrity with yourself.

Navigating your conscious awareness process is about putting what you have learned into practice, not only in the quiet stillness of your Faraday Cage, but in the midst of confusing and difficult situations in your life. It is about climbing back up when you fall off the cliff. It is about celebrating your ordinary state of being while manifesting extraordinary things through the co-creative process with the Source. What if you begin to see that your daily life is your practice arena for awakening? The events of your day provide you the space to embody your new, enlightened awareness. Whether you are dealing with your boss, your husband, your child, your mom, your sibling, or a stranger, it is your chance to practice conscious awareness. It is your opportunity to observe the observer and when things do not feel right, notice what is being triggered.

Having learned what we learned in this work, and having come this far, you should have the confidence not only that this is possible, but that you have the practical toolbox to ensure that you will be successful. Anytime you feel that your work is yielding negative results, your relationships are not smooth, or you are experiencing a negative emotion, it may be an indication that you are off-track. Ask yourself if it is connected to your Emotional Logo. If so, is it connected to the past rather than the present? It is in these moments that you can apply the Quickstep DANCE I'll be sharing in this chapter.

To illustrate the Quickstep DANCE, let's take the example of my friend Leo. After working at the same company for twenty-two years, without any warning, he was fired overnight because of an unfounded grievance against him from a long-standing troublemaker, who was smart enough to manipulate the manager and ended up being selected to replace Leo.

When Leo called me, he was devastated. He could not sleep or eat. Leo had always been proud of his achievements and had received a number of awards and accolades throughout his tenure with the company. He had been just two years away from getting a full retirement. Unfortunately, while being an accomplished professional, Leo was also a highly anxious individual who operated from fear. Through years of fear-based conditioning, his negative emotions and thoughts had developed negative pathways of pessimistic beliefs.

I visited Leo to offer my support to him and his family. His living room felt like a funeral parlor. Leo droned on and on about being the victim of a manipulator. He described how everybody had conspired against him to make him lose his job and his retirement. I asked Leo if he was interested in shifting the situation. He was open to doing so, given how intolerable his pain was. I could feel Leo's dismay and sincerity. Since we had limited time, I coached him through the Quickstep DANCE.

I asked Leo if he would close his eyes, breathe deeply, and relax for few minutes. I walked him through the breathing exercises and guided him to visualize his Clear Lagoon. Then I led him through each of the five stages in a simple sequence:

1. **Discover Your Emotions.** I asked Leo if he could open up the emotion bottled inside of him. What was it that he was feeling? Beyond the anger and despair, Leo discovered a deep fear. I asked him to localize this feeling sensation in his body, which he did—in his throat. Leo had derived his Emotional Logo in relationship to this devastating event in his life.

2. **Awaken to Your Beliefs.** Next, I asked Leo to liberate the belief behind this feeling by going back to his childhood and

tracing an instance of same emotion he was feeling. He was able to retrace this feeling back to his childhood in Italy— to the first time his mother scolded him and called him "Demonio." She told him that the "Basseta" would come and take him away because he failed a class at school. The "Bassetta" was a homeless beggar who lived close to their house, and Leo was terrified of her. That day, his mom was not yelling. She was calm and collected, which was unusual for her. This is when Leo realized that his mom was dead serious. She had packed up his clothes in a bag by the door. The raw emotion of fear made that Marker event stick in his mind, even though the threat was never carried out. It led to a belief that he was inadequate and undeserving.

3. **Name Your Patterns.** I asked Leo to look at the actions he had taken in his professional situation and to notice if they were part of his normal pattern. Because Leo deeply believed that he was inadequate and undeserving, his pattern had been to become a hero. He was afraid that people would discover that he was "demonio," or evil, so his survival strategy was to become "Sir Lancelot." He wanted to save his company from the manipulative, lazy troublemaker. Once his strategy failed, he was lost and did not know who he was. His shadow pattern came into play. His fear was crippling. He felt bitter and became vindictive against his boss. He was later dismissed, which was something he could not accept.

4. **Cancel Your Polarities.** I asked Leo to produce an antidote to his belief about himself— a list of times where he has been a great employee, a great partner, a great father. I asked him to find positive qualities for the troublemaker and overturn his beliefs about her. Then I asked him to turn the mirror around and see in himself similar qualities to those he

disliked in her and then cancel them out with genuine good qualities. He went through the same sequence with his boss. Through the cancelation of the negative charge, Leo was able to become neutral and shift his point of view about the situation.

5. **Embrace Your True Self.** Through this process, Leo was able to finally accept his dismissal without resisting it. Since he could not change the situation, he chose a new attitude toward it. He forgave himself, his boss, and the troublemaker and let go of his anger. By aligning himself with the light, he was able to connect to his own passion and rekindle the fire of his true self. Leo was able to give himself space to surrender to the way things had turned out. He was able to recognize his responsibility in the matter, and instead of reacting or acting out his pattern, he found the gold within the crisis. It turned out he had badly wanted to leave his company, but he had been afraid to make the move. Being laid off afforded him the opportunity to create his own business.

Two years later, Leo had become a prosperous entrepreneur and created one of the most successful medical-purchasing groups in the Midwest. He had connected to his deeper passion and was able to create value and wealth in his own life and in the life of people around him. Through aligning himself with the light and canceling the negative charge of his deep embedded emotions, he recognized his talent, expressed his passion and his uniqueness in the world, and found a way to contribute to the whole.

Exercise 14: The Quickstep DANCE

Please read the exercise thoroughly before you begin. For this exercise, you may want to try working without your notebook, so that you get used to going through the steps in your mind wherever you happen to be in the moment. The acronym DANCE will remind you of the steps.

Sit quietly and move into a state of relaxation using the Clear Lake visualization we created in chapter two (p. 20). Once you are established there, breathe deeper and deeper.

Think of a challenge you are going through right now and apply the Quickstep DANCE by following these five steps:

1. Discover what is in the space between the situation and you. What is the feeling you have about it? What is your inner conversation about it? What is your perception of what happened? Is there any emotion that is triggered about yourself as a result of it? If you are feeling an emotion right now, is it associated with your Emotional Logo? Acknowledge it.

2. Awaken to your limiting beliefs about yourself. Is there an undercurrent of negative conclusions about you being "not enough"? If you are feeling not good enough, not capable enough, not lovable enough, and so on, most likely, it is associated with your Identity Signature.

3. Name your Core Pattern and your Shadow Pattern. Did you act out of your Core Pattern or react with your Shadow one? Notice whether this incident is affecting your opinion about yourself. Are you judging yourself for what happened? What self are you being right now? Who are you identifying with, your Identity Signature or your true self? Notice the illusion.

4. Cancel the polarity of the experience. For each negative belief that is being triggered, think of its

genuine opposite. Think of all the facts that prove your point of view wrong, and cancel them. If you are feeling victimized by what happened, ask yourself what is your responsibility in the matter and cancel the victim point of view. Cancel the opposition from the experience and transcend the negativity.

5. **Embrace** your true self, the new space that you are in. Give yourself some time to love yourself without judgment. Shy away from repeating and rehearsing what happened, and tell your immediate friends and family that you need some time for yourself. Reignite your own light through recommitting yourself to your purpose, and let the universal light guide your next steps. At least one commitment to action should emerge from this step. It could be a recommitment to a project, a relationship, or an action in the world totally aligned with your true self.

Now visualize the dolphin in your Clear Lagoon leaping above the water and flipping over. Visualize the dolphin's flip in your situation by replacing the challenge with a new image that is the opposite of the situation at hand. For example, Leo visualized the dolphin flipping over, got inspired by it, and flipped his situation from being anxious and afraid to be without a job, to being happy, fulfilled, and loving his new freedom and opportunities. Breathe deeply and let it go. The dolphin's flip is a powerful and immediate image for transforming any situation at hand.

From now on, you can use this short sequence if you have a few minutes. If you don't even have time to go through all the steps, just move straight to the flip: imagine the contrary of what is occurring in your life right now. Breathe deeply, visualize your Clear Lagoon, and see the flip of the dolphin.

This powerful image will help you quickly shift any upset you are going through. If the situation persists, you can go back to the Quickstep DANCE process and go through the questions.

The most important part of the process is to step back or out and witness what is occurring from a distance. Whenever you feel the strong winds of emotion or you get caught in repetitive thought, patterns, or compulsive behaviors, it is essential to take a moment to breathe and self-witness your thoughts, feelings, emotions, and sensations. If this happens to you while at work or in the midst of some activity you can't stop, I suggest that you simply observe, take a couple of deep breaths, visualize the dolphin, and flip it. Then "file" the incident away for later—"bank" it, or "park" it, knowing that you only had time to temporarily shift, and not enough for a deep dive. Shifting the incident too quickly, before the feelings have been worked through, may not effectively cancel out the negative charge, especially if there is an underlying emotion at play. Bottling up those emotions is unhealthy, and they are likely to resurface when you are not expecting them. My personal experience is such that when I bank an incident to come back to it later, I put it in a box in my mind and set it aside. Then, during my evening meditation, I can retrieve it from the box, acknowledge the underlying emotion and belief below the surface, cancel it out, and clear my own space.

10 ALIGN YOUR PURPOSE WITH THE SOURCE

The meaning of life is to find your gift.
The purpose of life is to give it away.
—**Pablo Picasso**

Now that you have completed your journey of self-discovery, you have become whole again. You have integrated the fragmented pieces of your disowned self and united them consciously with your inner being. I hope this process has led you to a degree of clarity and freedom that you have not experienced before. That doesn't mean the journey is over, but you are now ready to express your passion in the world. You are prepared to dance in harmony with the universe.

Higher consciousness—whether you call it Source, Energy, Spirit, the Creative Force, the Evolutionary Impulse, God, or anything else—needs to express itself through our human experience. How do we share this connection to the Source when we experience it and tap into it?

That energy is translated into our actions in this world. We are the way the Source expresses itself! Therefore, now that you have passed through the five stages of the inner journey of conscious awareness, it is time to turn your attention to your expression in the world. You are ready to move from conscious awareness to contributing who you are to your family, your community, your society, and to the world you live in. When we align to our true selves, we align our minds to the universal mind. Your purpose becomes a contribution to life and to humanity. The more you contribute, the more you are contributed to. The more you give, the more you are given. You create a ripple effect in the water of life, a generous cycle of abundance.

Conscious awareness is no longer a concept leading you to become aware but a call for transforming your actions in the world. It is time to embark on the enactment of a higher vision of yourself in action—a vision that incorporates all of you as a whole, holy, integrated being and makes space for higher consciousness to manifest through you. As you open your heart to this higher consciousness and clear the inner space to accept it and receive it, your life may take on a whole different trajectory. Rather than looking outside of you—to other people or cultural values—to see who you want to be and where you want to go, you will start co-creating your destiny with the Source from the inside out by tuning in to your deepest essence and discovering your purpose.

Purpose can seem like a grandiose word, but it does not have to be something dramatic. Your purpose in life is certainly bigger than your false identity but is smaller than your true self. Your true self is connected to the universal energy of the Source that is bigger than all of us. Your purpose is just one single facet of the expression of that true self and its contribution to the whole. Each one of us on this planet, through our uniqueness, contributes our portion to the whole. And each particle of us contains the whole within it.

Whenever we are inspired about something we are doing, creating, or contributing to the world, we are connecting to the Source through our passion. We are vibrating at a higher frequency, our consciousness expands, and latent forces dormant within us come alive and seek to be expressed through us for a higher purpose. The key to becoming an expression of the Source in action is to simply make use of the basic talent that was given to us by the Source energy itself.

Every human being is born with some particular talent, affinity, or strength. That's part of our human birthright. It's not a particular role or mode of expression, and the same talent might manifest itself in multiple ways throughout a lifetime. It can develop and evolve with time, but what remains constant is the quality of that natural talent. It is that thing you do easily, effortlessly, that excites you and makes your heart beat faster. That thing that you wake up for in the morning and makes you enthusiastic and motivated. That thing that does not make you tired. That thing that people around you praise you for and remember you by. That is your talent—your contribution to the universe.

An interesting example of how talent can manifest itself in one's life is my friend's son, Rafael. I have known him since he was a baby. Ever since he came into this world, he has been an extremely perceptive person, especially as relating to human nature. He has always had the ability to capture, analyze, and perceive many different human cues at once and without effort or conscious thought. While he was still a toddler, I recall going into a store with him and the conversation that ensued. We were in line waiting to check out when the male cashier said to the woman in line in front of us, "How can I help you today, pretty lady?" Rafael did not react right away but waited until it was our turn to check out. Before the cashier could greet us, Rafael looked at him and said, "Why did you call that lady pretty if you really didn't think she was?" In witnessing an exchange that lasted only eight words, Rafael's natural instinct was not to listen to the words themselves but instead to capture the emotions, expressions, and non-verbal cues present around him.

Because this was a skill that came naturally to him, he never thought of it as a "talent." In fact, he spent many years searching for his calling in life. Most of us grow up believing that talents are skills that you can obviously see, like singing, throwing a ball into a hoop, dancing, or acting. Most of us do not look at the invisible talents we each possess. Some of us may get lucky and fall into a path that reinforces and highlights our innate skills, but most of us have to first identify our talents, tie them into our passion, and create a path that will not only utilize these skills, but also help us refine and expand them.

It took many years, many different fields of study, and many different self-discovery "sessions" for Rafael to finally understand that his talent was truly in reading and understanding people. He then learned to create a space for people to share and express even more than they thought possible. He has since built a successful career in helping individuals match with their true calling in life, find their passion, and create their professional path by cutting through the clutter of traditional conversation while focusing on the non-verbal and subconscious cues that surround them. He is one of the fortunate individuals who discovered his "talent," embraced it, and in turn, found a way to share it with the world.

Your basic talent is your entry point to expressing your higher purpose. It really does not matter what avenue you choose through which to express it, so long as you are doing what you are most passionate about. Since passion is an emotion, it has an incredibly positive charge that can move mountains, provided you don't try to micromanage it, block it, or become too specific about the ways you want to direct it. If you align your passion to the universal energy, the sky becomes your limit. It aligns with the creative force of the universe, the permanent impulse behind every life form. Your higher purpose, once activated, will be the engine of your joy and happiness. Let it be, let it soar, let it direct you, and don't let yourself try to control it or contain it, as it is larger than your ego. Once you grasp that you are simply a conduit, a space for it to manifest through, then you become the co-creator of who you are becoming with it.

This role allows energy and passion to flourish and provides a clear and clean space in which it can manifest. Your role is to get out of its way and listen. You are the space in which it can happen. However, I am not suggesting that you be passive. Being passive, like being very controlling, puts you at risk of losing your connection to it. While your purpose never dies, your connection to it may be broken or blocked.

So, what is your role once you connect to it? First, you have to trust your inner voice. You have to have faith in where it is taking you, even if you can't control its trajectory. And you have to *act* on it. Action is the manifestation of spirit. If you don't act, it simply ceases to exist.

You also have a responsibility to constantly clear your space within for it to manifest in its highest degree of potential and clarity. We have all heard stories about great teachers or leaders who fell apart or abused their power because they did not keep their inner space clean. The story of Jeffrey earlier in this book is a great illustration of this challenge. Jeffrey was a great teacher to his students, yet he fell short toward himself and the closest people to him. People like him have helped others but neglected their own selves, whether it was their bodies, their mental or physical health, or their spiritual health. Too often, they identified with their false selves without realizing it.

These great men and women were in touch with their higher purpose, they had faith in it, and they listened to it. Their downfall was that they allowed their own egos to take over. While they were probably initially in touch with that passion, that spark of the Source that propelled them to become inspirational and famous, fame gave them the possibility of rebuilding their false identities, which they then confused with their true selves. They clogged up their conscious awareness. Yes, it happens a lot. Once we are aware of these dangers, it may help to keep re-sourcing ourselves from the pure river of humility and gratitude. It helps to be reminded that we are simply conduits for higher intelligence to use us. Recognizing our false identities needs to become a constant practice as part of the conscious-awareness process, as this process is a continuous one and not an end in itself.

Engaging in regular conscious-awareness practices is essential to keeping your conduit clean and manifesting your highest purpose to its ultimate potentials without tainting it with ego. Acting on your inner voice and singing your song is not only a desirable outcome; it is a deliberate responsibility on your part to allow your higher purpose to manifest through you. Your higher purpose is part of the higher consciousness of the universe. This higher consciousness is constantly in motion; it pushes its way into the space through a universal impulse that takes a form of energy in the physical world.

What happens if you don't create a space for the higher consciousness to flow through you? That impulse will not be stopped. It is vibrating with or without you. If you don't align yourself with it, it will find a way to be expressed elsewhere. But the loss is that your uniqueness will not be voiced and contributed to the cosmic dance of life. Your potentiality will stay dormant, and you may not be participating fully in the process of co-creation with the Source.

Aligning with our higher purpose connects us to the emotion of joy and passion emanating from the Source. We draw our creativity from the infinite field of possibilities. We feel part of something higher than us. This connection calls us to action in the world. We start expressing our talents with creativity and passion. We become united with our essence, and we love ourselves for that. For instance, since I was very young, I have been an avid seeker to understand the meaning of the universe and how it applies to me. I have found a certain ease with demystifying the big picture of our existence and rendering it more accessible to others and to myself. Writing this book is the expression of this passion, and sharing it with you is contributing my talent to the universe.

Once you find a way to express your passion, for the sole purpose of contributing to the universe—whether you earn a living from it or you do it on a volunteer basis—you will get in touch with your higher purpose in life. If you do this wholeheartedly, it won't be long before you may find that you can earn your living from your talent, because sooner or later, you will excel at it. Once again, your life's purpose is not one particular role or expression. The purpose is your essence, and it remains the same whether you express it through coaching in career development, helping your neighbors, writing a book, singing, campaigning for political change, cooking, or doing life's daily work. When you stay present to your unique talent and you reduce the space between your real self and your purpose, you find yourself expressing it in whatever you are doing.

When you are connected to the light, you will sooner or later align with your sense of purpose. It may be something you are already doing in your work, in your creative pursuits, in your passions, in your relationships. Or it may be something you need to seek out. At times, we have to break away from what is familiar to us and embark on a hero's journey. Finding your sense of purpose might be the path of a lonesome warrior, because it may conflict with the life of people around you. But in reality, you will not be lonesome inside, because you will find fullness and meaning for your life through doing what you love the most. Once you start expressing your unique brilliance, you will begin to create a life beyond your wildest dreams. If you allow the force of the Source to direct your life, you can trust that it will lead you to positive things. But if you become too specific about controlling your essence or get caught up in materialistic desires or fears, you will meddle with its flow, dilute it, and lose its focus. Your purpose will become elusive and obscure again. Therefore, it is one thing to connect with your purpose, but it takes a constant alignment to keep living it in your daily life and get out of its way in order to allow it to take you to places you have never dreamt of.

If you are in touch with your purpose, you will find a way to express it, even when circumstances seem to conspire to prevent you. My dry cleaner Sue is from Korea. Her English is very basic, despite the fact that she has been living in the States for a long time. I love dropping off my laundry at her store. Every time she sees me, she flashes a beautiful smile and tells me something about my life. Interestingly, what she says is usually not only true, but also something personal I have never shared with her. Sue's talent is that she is a very perceptive and intuitive person. But the circumstances of her life are such that she cannot earn a living from her talent. Nonetheless, she practices her mission and connects to her higher purpose by helping her clients through simple conversations as they drop off and collect their laundry.

Connecting to Source will lead you to connect to your own passion and ignite your own fire. Your light will shine, and it will lead your way and inspire others to ignite their own fire as well. You will be inspired and inspiring. The purpose of your conscious-awareness journey is to allow you to unearth the full expression of who you are and share it with others and the universe. The more consciously aware you become, the more you are able to put your uniqueness in the service of the whole. You contribute to humanity through allowing spirit to use you as a vehicle of communication.

Navigating your self-discovery means expressing your higher purpose in action in every arena of your life. You become attuned to your inner being and to your higher potential at the same time. You allow the higher energy of the Source to flow through you and express itself, aligning your mind, your body, and your actions so that you are expressing yourself fully. You become self-actualized. Giving is really receiving ten times over; you start finding a true sense of purpose and a meaning in being yourself. You become centered in the light of the universe. This will allow your flame to be sacred and to regenerate itself. It will be an endless flame that will continue to shine beyond your lifetime because of the impact you had on your environment and those around you. Again, this may sound grandiose, but the expression of your purpose does not need to be an ambitious or large-scale action. When you are aligned with your purpose, whether great or small, you become the hero of your own journey. You will never be bored again, but you will reignite your fire every time you put your passion in action.

No matter what your purpose is, connecting to it and contributing it around you will move your evolution forward in a conscious way. Your goals will become aligned with your purpose. You will feel a sense of fulfillment and joy through living a purpose-driven life. Living this joy and expanding it is allowing your own light to shine. This joy is contagious to people around you, and you will start affecting them in many ways.

Like a dolphin skimming the waves, you will be dancing, having fun, contributing, and expressing life fully by expressing your full potentials. Your originality becomes your new Logo, and your past Verdict is silenced and canceled out. Whenever it resurges, it will be short-lived, and your bounce-back time will be reduced. The space between you and the Source becomes smaller and smaller. In time, you will be merging with it, not knowing where you end and Source begins, especially if you are expressing yourself with full authenticity and integrity. You surrender to who you really are and allow your full expression to manifest in the world. You will be able to clean the space between you and pure consciousness every time it becomes cluttered, which will allow the current of the cosmos, the universal impulse, to flow through you continuously.

Inspired? Ready to release your passion and express the universal energy through your unique form? Let's dive in and do an exercise to get in touch with your basic talent and your purpose.

EXERCISE 15: FIND YOUR BASIC TALENT, WHICH LEADS YOU TO YOUR PURPOSE

Please read the exercise thoroughly and write the questions in your notebook before proceeding.

Open your notebook to your Identity Signature page and review it before you start your breathing and visualization exercise.

STEP 1

Sit quietly and move into a state of relaxation using the Clear Lagoon visualization we created in chapter two (p. 20). Once you are established there, breathe deeper and deeper.

STEP 2

Call upon your child image as you are sitting under the tree by your Clear Lagoon.

STEP 3

You may also want to call in your higher self or visualize a spiritual guide, such as someone you believe in or a trusted teacher, if you have one. If not, you can think of someone dear to you who has crossed over to the spirit world. Breathe deeply and connect to your higher self or spirit guide; ask if he or she would be willing to help you.

STEP 4

Breathe deeper and deeper and ask yourself the following questions:

a. *What is the thing I loved doing when I was young that I still enjoy doing now?*

b. *What is the thing that I love most in my life?*

c. *What is the thing that I will regret most if I die without having done it in my life?*

d. *What is the thing that brings me alive—that I can spend hours doing without noticing the time pass?*

e. *What is the thing that I am yearning to do, the desire I have not fulfilled yet?*

f. *What is the thing that I am great at? That comes to me easily, effortlessly?*

g. *What is the thing that, when I do it, I feel I am contributing to the world—the thing that will leave the world a better place when I depart this earth?*

h. *What is the thing that I am unique at and I feel I can do better than anybody else?*

i. *What is my deepest heart's desire? If I had a magic wand, what would I create in my life right now?*

j. *What is the deepest song that my soul is longing to sing?*

Read through your answers and notice whether you had the same answer more than once. If not, see if there is a general theme to your answers. The general theme points you toward your purpose. The things you are talented at indicate the expressions of your purpose.

STEP 5

Close your eyes and try to visualize that special talent of yours. Feel the feeling of doing it in the world. What will be the impact of your actions on the world as you know it? Who will benefit from your talent? Feel the emotion of success that comes when you are singing your deepest song. Visualize yourself doing it at a large scale. Rehearse your song. Exaggerate the feeling of happiness.

STEP 6

Visualize the white light showering you while you are singing your song. Visualize a festival of light performing in your honor to thank you for your unique contribution to life. Visualize your higher self or your spirit guide manifesting through you as you surrender to the flow. Start dancing with the flow; sing louder and louder. Breathe deeply. Open your eyes. Thank your spirit guide, then your inner child, and express your gratitude to the Source.

11 DANCE LIKE A DOLPHIN

*The more you see yourself as what you'd like to become,
and act as if what you want is already there, the more
you'll activate those dormant forces that will collaborate
to transform your dream into your reality.*
—Wayne Dyer

Creating this process and writing this book has been a dream come true for me, and one of the most enlightening experiences I have ever had in my life. I was excited to be able to deepen my vision, engrave its meaning on the page, and share it with you. I always felt that despite having received this vision, it really did not belong to me—it was as if I was hoarding something that I did not know what to do with. It took me a long time to decipher it and then to use it to shift my relationship with my thoughts, beliefs, patterns, and shadow, to clear my space within and reconnect to the light.

And now, here I am. Eyes closed, meditating this morning, the way I start almost every day. Acknowledging the many years of my past: the ups, downs, and everything in between. Grateful for the many roles I played and for the gift of my life. My deepest connection to myself comes directly from my journey into conscious awareness. As long as I am connected to the supreme light of consciousness, nothing is missing in my life. I can now say that the little girl in me who once lost her dad in his physical form gained the meaning of life through her losses. She learned how to integrate her broken pieces and change the name of the game in a moment of awareness.

Connecting my deep purpose in life to consciousness itself is my greatest empowerment, and contributing it to you, the reader, is my greatest joy. The Source inspires me to inspire you. I imagine you connecting to your essence and, in turn, inspiring others.

I am honored to have accompanied you on this journey. I hope that through your deep dive, you have rekindled your inner light, awakened to your greatness, and expanded your conscious awareness. I hope that you will continue your dance of consciousness, connect to the universal light, and share it with the world with passion, joy, and love. Now that you have participated in this beautiful dance of awakening, my greatest wish for you is that you will keep it alive and practice, practice, practice your awareness as often as you can.

I recommend engaging in daily practices to enhance, clear, and deepen your awareness. It takes a long time to break a habit. Despite your awakening, your patterns can and will sneak back when your defenses are low. In order to reprogram your subconscious, practices and rituals are helpful. Any change involves learning through repetition. Research has shown that it takes a minimum of twenty-one days of continuous programming to change a habit or replace a learned behavior. Appendix 1 includes some of the practices that I find particularly useful for reprogramming habits, interrupting patterns, and manifesting the life I want, while staying connected to the greater consciousness.

Remember, the process of conscious awareness is never finished. Don't be surprised if you are confronted with new challenges and opportunities for learning just at those moments in your life when you think you have arrived at a goal or achieved a dream. This happens to me often. In fact, I experienced such a moment just as I was coming to the end of writing this book.

After finishing the writing and going through the first edits, I had a major setback. I was confronted with the betrayal of a close friend of many years who suddenly became vindictive toward me. It was a side of her that I had never witnessed before, or maybe refused to see. I found myself wondering, why now? Why, at this moment, when my work was almost ready to be handed to the world, did I have to face such an intense challenge?

One night, I was flipping through my TV while my Verdict clamored for attention in my head. *I am not capable enough to flip my own state of being!* All the old fears, anxieties, and insecurities were arising again. *Who am I to be writing this book? One little challenge and I am trapped again!*

Then, as I changed the channel, I came across Oprah Winfrey interviewing Paulo Coelho, author of *The Alchemist*. Paulo was saying that when you are ready with your dream, the universe will test you with all its power to see if you learned the lessons. Suddenly, I understood what was happening to me. It became clear that I had to go through my final test before handing my dream to you.

I stayed in my Faraday Cage for a whole day and canceled out the polarities of the circumstances that had been handed to me. I recognized my responsibilities in the matter at hand and shifted my awareness to accepting the personality of my friend with love and gratitude for the lesson she was teaching me. Indeed, the learning was precious: her shadow was a mirror for me to see mine. Once I saw the piece of my shadow pattern that I was refusing to see, I was able to shed light on the relationship and accept it for what it is. I made peace with myself and with my friend. This energy cleared my inner space, and my work on this book moved forward, just as the universe became ready for it.

Sometimes your challenges may be large and dramatic; other times, they may just be subtle hints that something is slightly wrong. As you deepen your practice of conscious awareness, you will learn to be attuned to even the smallest shifts in your inner space. You are dancing the dance of the Source, like a dolphin leaping above the waves, and when the beat is off, your conscious awareness will alert you and will get you back on the beat if you listen. Your true self knows the difference between your Patterns, your Shadows, your Verdicts, and your limiting beliefs. By continuing to practice the five stages you've learned, you will be able to quickly dissolve the conditioning of your past experiences, change your mental framework, and shift your consciousness. In this, you are allowing yourself to expand beyond the boundaries of your identity.

When you live with conscious awareness, the space within becomes sacred. You will feel as if you are vibrating with the same vibration as the universal drum. You will savor the sweetness of the moment and swim in the infinite love and gratitude of the universe. There will be no other place you want to be and nothing else you wish to do except to listen to the vibration of that universal energy. Your heart is beating with it; you feel the surges of infinite love toward yourself and toward the world. You accept the shadows as part of the whole and still love them from a place of neutrality. Indeed, conscious awareness is beyond being positive. It is about being authentic and integrating our wholeness. Once we integrate our whole self, we become whole with the universe, and this wholeness becomes the access to oneness consciousness, as our wholeness is now in harmony with the wholeness of the universe. We are all part of the same essence.

This state of connectedness with your true nature allows you to love others and yourself from a place of total acceptance. Your true self recognizes the true self in the other person and treats others the same way you want to be treated. It connects to them with the same authenticity with which you connect to yourself. Love, gratitude, and compassion become your natural expression. In this way, conscious awareness has a powerfully transformative potential not just for you, but also for the world around you.

Imagine a world in which many of us were living in this heightened state of awareness and connectedness to the Source of all life. Imagine how different life would be and what a difference we could make. When we share our expanded consciousness with authenticity, purpose, passion, compassion, and gratitude, this cycle of positive energy becomes contagious in the world; it expands and perpetuates itself, and it generates an ocean of goodness and love in which you play like a dolphin. Imagine how you could effortlessly swim, flip above the waves, and dance with love and inner joy.

To conclude this book, I offer you this poem, along with my deepest gratitude:

CONSCIOUS AWARENESS

In the mind of the Source I was resting peacefully
In a breath of life it uttered my name gracefully
Out of an undifferentiated field of light I appeared suddenly
The singer and the song originating from the One, separated gently

The song loud and strong left the field, longing to return to the
    Source instantly
Now the prodigal daughter I became; I must make my own
    discovery
I got lost and confused at times; afraid due to a verdict that was not
    ordained consciously
The storehouse of nature is filled with good, but this good is locked
    from me momentarily

In my deep dive only my clear eyes could witness my beliefs and
    patterns eagerly
In a leap of consciousness, I discovered that the key to this door was
    held inside of me
Whatever my mind perceived it could conceive it limitlessly
I went beyond my belief and expanded my vision

My ego melted in the fire of love; its scattered ashes returned to
the One
A pure light within my center is now revealed to me
No story can be told except from the universal mind beyond eternity
I awakened my true self and unveiled my purpose in life consciously

I received the light and now search for it in every being equally
Steps forward and back are the name of the dance, when I separate
from the Source
I flip my move like the dolphin and continue my dance indefinitely
With the jubilee of light, I continue to sing my song, which becomes
the singer ultimately

APPENDIX 1
CONSCIOUS AWARENESS PRACTICE TOOLS

In addition to the exercises included in this book, I recommend engaging in daily practices to enhance, clear, and deepen your awareness. Here are some of the practices that I find particularly useful for reprogramming habits, interrupting patterns, and manifesting the life you want, while staying connected to the greater consciousness.

1. MEDITATION AND VISUALIZATION

This includes your breathing exercises and your Clear Lagoon visualization. I recommend that you practice the breathing exercises and the visualization of your Clear Lagoon, morning and night, as part of a meditation. Here are two simple formats you can use for a ten-minute meditation following this visualization:

> **Morning:** Take ten minutes to visualize your day before you get out of bed while still in the alpha state. After doing your breathing exercises, visualize your Clear Lagoon, and invoke the light. Then rehearse your day in your mind; visualize a positive outcome for each of your planned activities and end with a positive affirmation of your choice. I usually end it with the following affirmation: "I am

grateful, protected, and empowered by the light."
Count from one to ten, open your eyes softly, and
carry this feeling with you throughout your day.

Evening: As soon as you get into bed, start your
breathing exercises, visualize your Clear Lake,
and invoke the light. Now, review your day. As
you are reviewing the events from your day,
cancel the polarity of any negative experiences. Be
thankful for any positive experiences. End with
the affirmation: "I know I am grateful, protected,
and loved unconditionally." Stay with the feelings
of peacefulness. If you are practicing this deep-
relaxation technique at the end of your day, you do
not need to count from one to ten when you are
done—you can simply allow your mind to remain
in this pleasant state of relaxation and keep your
eyes closed as you drift into sleep.

2. Pattern Interruption

If, through the DANCE process, you detect a pattern that you would
like to interrupt or replace, use the Clear Lagoon visualization to
create a state of deep relaxation, then visualize the current pattern
that you would like to change with as much detail as possible, and
frame it with a wooden frame in your mind. Then imagine the new
pattern that you would like to create. Feel the emotion of the new
pattern; visualize it with as much detail as you can, including its
outcome in your life. Then frame it with the light of your choice.
Continue breathing deeply. Imagine the dolphin's flip. With his flip,
he replaces the old pattern with the new one and merges it with
the light. Feel a radiant light engulf you; feel it become part of you.
Thank the light and the dolphin, release it, count from one to ten,
and open your eyes gently.

3. REHEARSAL MANIFESTATION

If you want to manifest something in your life, this technique is very effective. It involves the mental rehearsal of future events that anchors your future vision of yourself to positive emotions through visualization techniques. It programs the subconscious to bring forth a desired intention into reality, either by seeing yourself on a screen or by imagining an experience as if it were happening right now and feeling its emotion in the present moment as you are in a deep relaxation state. If you are constantly visualizing things going right while in a deep relaxed state, you create a believable scenario for your unconscious mind, and you start getting positive outcomes that override your perception that things are going wrong in your life.

Begin by visualizing your Clear Lagoon. Then think of a past happy event in your life. Recall the emotion of the happy event. Connect to that feeling of happiness. Relive the event with your five senses. Get in touch with it. Connect to it through your breath. Feel the emotion of that event. Then project yourself on a screen in front of you. Rehearse all the steps of the future event you want to manifest, while you connect the positive feeling of your past happy event to it. Visualize the successful outcome. Visualize your goal already attained, whether it is writing a book or buying a house or manifesting a relationship. See yourself having attained the goal or manifested your desire on the screen. Describe yourself with all five senses if possible. Feel the emotion of happiness. Cover yourself with the light. Thank the light and release it. Start counting from one to ten. Open your eyes gently and repeat: "I am in complete harmony with the light."

4. AFFIRMATIONS

Affirmations are powerful. The more you repeat them, the more you end up believing in them. Affirmations are based on the principles of positive thinking. The pitfall with affirmations, as with all forms of positive thinking, is that despite the old adage "fake it until you make it," if affirmations are kept on the surface level and you don't deeply believe in them, you won't make it. You will most likely fail and go back to your old thinking patterns again. If, however, your affirmations are anchored in positive beliefs at the subconscious level, repeating them can generate an unprecedented positive effect. If, after completing this process, you still believe the negative thoughts about yourself, you will need to repeat the process while doing your affirmations. What we believe is true becomes true. The mind script that is welded in your subconscious will get in the way of attracting the life you want.

For example, if you are using a positive affirmation to reach a goal of losing weight, you have to believe that you can lose weight. The affirmation "I am losing weight, I am eating healthy, I feel better in my clothes," may feel good to repeat, but unless you change your thinking and your underlying beliefs about your ability to attain the goal, it will not be effective. If your underlying belief is that you can't lose weight, you may revert to your old pattern and give up on yourself. Therefore, I recommend that for each affirmation, you may want to check in with yourself and notice if you are running a sabotaging program underneath the surface that could override the positive affirmation. In that case, I would recommend that you go back to the Quickstep DANCE and apply the flip of the dolphin to shift your belief before proceeding with your affirmation.

I suggest that you end each meditation with a positive affirmation. I recommend that you tie in your affirmation to your Verdict. It should be the antidote to your Verdict. For example, if your Verdict is "I am not lovable," your daily affirmation should be "I am loved unconditionally."

5. Protection and Healing Meditation

This is a meditation that you can practice if you want to heal yourself from pain. Go to your Clear Lagoon. As you are invoking the light, make sure to concentrate it in the area of your pain. Increase the feeling of pain and then let go. Breathe in the healing energy and let go of the pain. With the light, caress the organ that is painful. Visualize yourself totally healed. Tell yourself that you are loved unconditionally as a whole, including your Verdict and your Shadow. Feel the healing light all around you and in you. You are swimming in the light of love. The healing love is enveloping you. Cover yourself with a pyramid of light. Identify with the light; merge with it. Thank the light for your healing, and let go. Count from one to ten and open your eyes gently. Affirm: "I am well, healthy, whole, and complete."

In addition to these practices, here are some final suggestions for practices and attitudes you can incorporate into your daily life.

Live in the present and be present to the moment and other people. Each emotion is a doorway that will lead to the expansion of your own being. Accept and become a space for people and situations as they become your teachers on your awareness path. Be compassionate and loving toward yourself and others.

Be conscious of the power of your language. Pay attention to the way you express yourself. Every time you use negative language, try to catch yourself and change it into positive forms. Language creates and affects your subconscious. By repeating positive language, you will end up changing your attitude.

Cultivate an attitude of gratitude; be grateful for and to everything in your life.

Create meaningful relationships with like-minded individuals you can connect to, who are authentic enough to empower you on your journey.

Spend time every day practicing your talents and following your passion—if not through your work, then through your hobbies.

Whatever you give attention to in your life has the potential to grow. It attracts more of itself. Even if you start by dedicating a few minutes each day to your basic purpose, it will grow and expand, and one day, it will become your sole playground. You make space for your future self to occur, and your future self starts calling you and manifesting in your life.

Become the Observer of the *I*—learn to step back and observe yourself from a place of detachment; bring conscious awareness to what is driving your actions. This is something you can do at anytime during your day. Every time you catch yourself having a negative thought about yourself or acting out a negative pattern, stop and ask yourself this question: Which self am I identifying with or enacting right now? Is it my false identity or my true self? If you catch yourself in a negative pattern, just acknowledge it, let go of your opinion about it, cancel its polarity by creating its opposite, and realign yourself with the light within you.

ENDNOTES

1   Chopra, Deepak, *The Seven Spiritual Laws of Success* (New World Library/ Amber-Allen Publishing; 1994) p. 1

2   Tolle, Eckhart, *A New Earth,* (Penguin, 2008) p. 53

3   Lipton, Bruce, *The Biology of Belief* (Hay House, 2008), p. xv

4   "Feeling Our Emotions: An Interview with Antonio R. Damasio by Manuela Lenzen," in *Scientific American Mind* April 2005. http://www. scientificamerican.com/article/feeling-our-emotions/ Accessed June 2014

5   Karla McLaren, "Is It A Feeling Or Is It An Emotion?" http://karlamclaren. com/is-it-a-feeling-or-is-it-an-emotion/ Accessed June 2014

6   Brown, Michael, *The Presence Process,* (Namaste Publishing, Vancouver and Beaufort Books New York, 2005) p. 213

7   Debbie Ford in an interview with Oprah Winfrey, February 2012, http:// nhne-pulse.org/debbie-ford-tells-oprah-she-has-cancer/ Accessed June 2014

8   In Paul, S.K, (Ed.) *The Complete Poems of Rabindranath Tagore's Gitanjali: Texts and Critical Evaluation,* (Sarup & Sons, 2006) p. 144

9   Klein, Jeff, *Working for Good: Making a Difference While Making a Living* (Sounds True, Inc. 2009) p. 57

10 Tolle, Eckhart, *A New Earth,* (Penguin Group, New York, 2006) p. 9

11 Wesselman, Hank and Kuykendall, Jill, *Spirit Medicine: Healing in the Sacred Realms* (Hay House, Inc., 2004) p.113

12 Quoted in Anderson, Ray S. "Spiritual caregiver as secular sacrament" (Jessica Kingsley, 2004) p.66

CPSIA information can be obtained at www.ICGtesting.com
Printed in the USA
LVOW07s1213180815

450475LV00002B/5/P